M000280388

How To Do It All

The Revolutionary Plan to Create a Full, Meaningful Life—While Only *Occasionally* Wanting to Poke Your Eyes Out With a Sharpie

By Linda Formichelli

Published by Renegade Writer Press
PO Box 12
Nutting Lake, MA 01865

Copyright © Linda Formichelli, 2016
All rights reserved.

ISBN: 978-0-9973468-0-0

No part of this publication may be reproduced, stored in a retrieval system, or transmitted in any form or by any means, electronic, mechanical, recording or otherwise, without the prior written permission of the author.

DISCLAIMER: This book is designed to provide information only on creating a full, enjoyable life. This information is provided and sold with the knowledge that the publisher and author do not offer any legal or other professional advice. In the case of a need for any such expertise consult with the appropriate professional. This book does not contain all information available on the subject. This book has not been created to be specific to any individual's or organization's situation or needs. Every effort has been made to make this book as accurate as possible; however, there may be typographical and or content errors; therefore, this book should serve only as a general guide, and not as the ultimate source of subject information. The author and publisher shall have no liability or responsibility to any person or entity regarding any loss or damage incurred, or alleged to have incurred, directly or indirectly, by the information contained in this book.

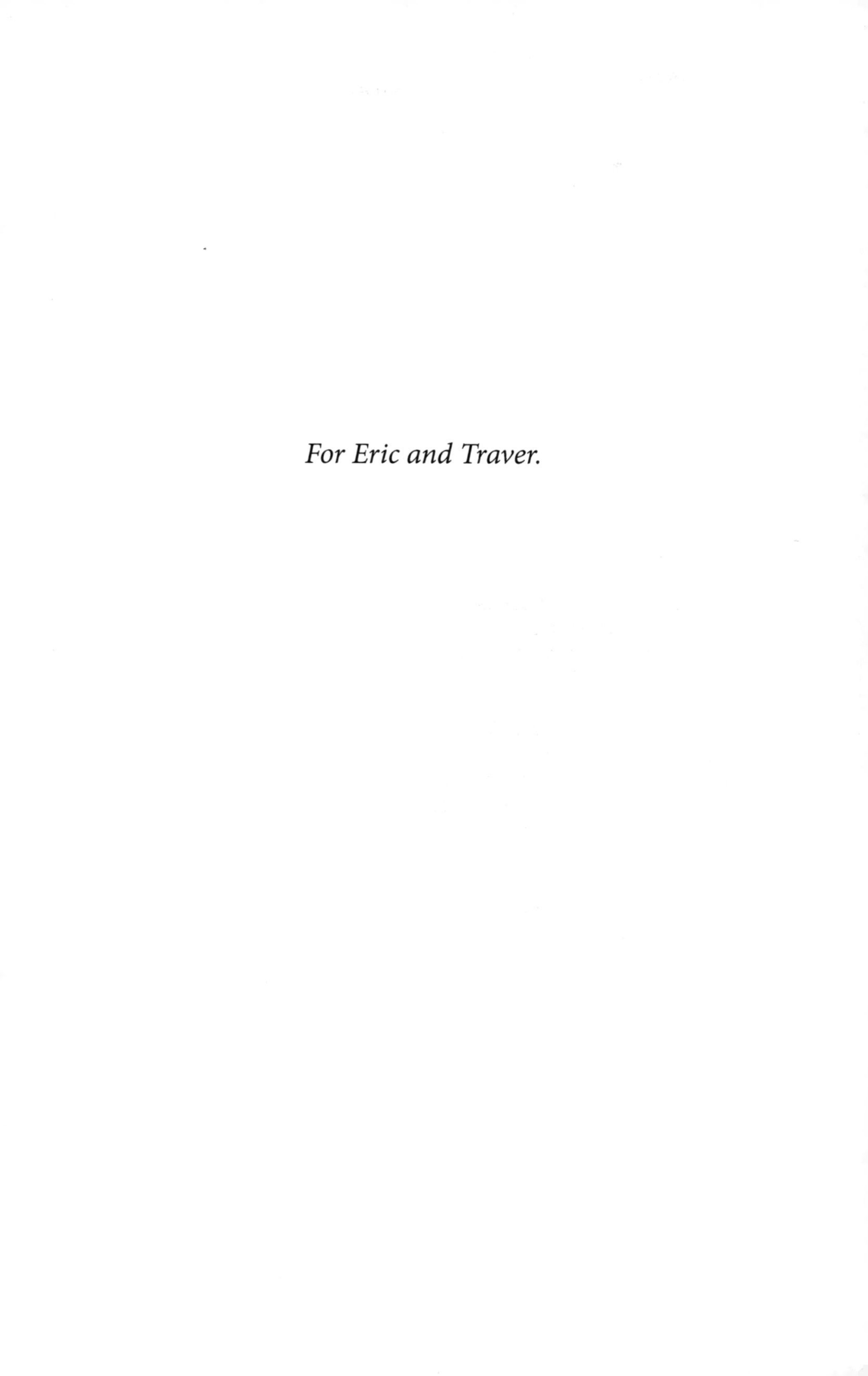

For Eric and Traver.

Table of Contents

How to Read This Book

First, make sure your e-reader is turned on or that your print book is open. (Do not get these mixed up!) Also be sure you're holding your device or book right-side up. Then, start at the upper left-hand corner of the page and read the words from left to right, working your way down the page…

Okay, okay. I always think those *how to read this book* instructions are kind of idiotic, but I do want to use this opportunity to assure you there is no right way to read this book. I arranged the chapters in a certain order because I feel readers will get the most out of the book this way. For example, the *Do-It-All Plan* doesn't appear until the final third of the book because I think it's important for readers to learn all the motivational and time management strategies, and get a boost of encouragement and inspiration, before diving into the Plan.

But you may feel compelled to skip right to the *Do-It-All Plan*, and that's fine, too. Seeing what's in store for the next chunk of your life should get you revved up, excited, and maybe even a little scared—but in a good way. Then you can come back and read about the strategies that will make your Plan a reality. So if you want to skip ahead, and then come back to the explanations and advice, then skip away!

Some Housekeeping Notes

From now on, I'll be abbreviating the adjective *Do-It-All* as *D-I-A*. So when I talk about your D-I-A Plan, I mean your Do-It-All Plan. And when I say we're looking to create a D-I-A life, I mean a Do-It-All life.

The D-I-A Plan is divided into 12 *Desires* I chose after speaking with women about what they wish they could be doing in their lives. If a

Desire doesn't resonate with you, or if there's one you want to pursue that isn't listed here, you can choose your own.

The 12 Desires are:

1. Love Your Looks
2. Travel
3. Create an Amazing Home
4. Cross a Finish Line
5. Entertain
6. Volunteer
7. Write
8. Become Well-Read
9. Start a Side Hustle
10. Gain Mad Skills
11. Grow Your Spiritual Practice
12. Do More Stuff With the People You Love

You'll choose a *Goal* for each Desire. These depend on what the Desire is and what it means to you. For example, for you, *Volunteer* may mean doing microvolunteering online, or it may mean joining the Peace Corps. Whatever you decide, this is your Goal for that Desire.

If you're stuck, I offer three *Levels* of Goals you can pursue. You can use any of these Goals if you're feeling stuck picking one of your own, as I selected Goals that are fairly accessible in terms of price and availability. For example, if you don't know what kind of athletic event you want to compete in for *Cross a Finish Line*, you can simply go with my Level 1 Goal—*Train for and run a 5k*. If you're pining for something more challenging, Level 2 (*Train for and run a half marathon*) and Level 3 (*Train for and run a marathon*) come into play. These races are ubiquitous, cheap to enter, and free to train for, which is why I recommend them if you're stuck for ideas.

This book comes with a free downloadable packet of printable *Worksheets*. To get these, visit www.therenegadewriter.com/D-I-AWorksheets.

In case you prefer to use your journal, or create your own Worksheets, at the end of this book you'll find an Appendix with a simple list of all of the Worksheets and the questions/prompts on each one.

The Do-It-All Manifesto

On New Year's Eve, 2015, I made a list of what I had done in the past year. Some of the highlights included going on trips with my family to Japan, Disney World, and four countries in Europe; running two profitable businesses; hosting three foreign exchange students; reading 32 books; speaking at a conference; writing a book, 40 blog posts, and two feature articles; hosting parties, dinners, and game nights; volunteering; practicing yoga and meditation; and of course, taking care of my family, pets, and home.

When I read over the final list, which had over 40 items, I was gobsmacked. We're a middle-class family with two working parents and a kid, and usually an exchange student, too. How had I accomplished all of that without going broke...or crazy?

Well, maybe I went a *little* crazy. There were times where I was so stressed that I felt ill. There were times I cried with exhaustion. But was it all worth it? *Hell yes*!

Read any blog, magazine, or book aimed at women and the common refrain is: "You have so much to do! You need to simplify your life and say no to things you really don't want to do. And ask your husband to clean the bathroom, you poor thing, so you can have 15 minutes to yourself. Now, take out your gratitude journal and write about how grateful you are that you can walk and breathe." Ick.

Would you rather look back on a year that was full of fun, adventure—and, yes, some stress—or remember a year where you floated through your days stress-free, but that's pretty much all you did?

The women's media also spout BS like, "Relax your standards on housecleaning" and "Your friends shouldn't care what your house looks like." But what if, like me, you want to enjoy a clean and attractive house?

Like, for yourself? What if creating a relaxing, clutter-free, joyful space is important for you and your family?

Then there's the ubiquitous, "Here's how to put on your makeup and do your hair in 1.3 seconds!" The media encourages women, especially moms, to spend time on their hair and makeup, but then they always push the time-saving element. What if you *want* to spend time looking good? What if you want an hour at the salon every month, taking care of a high-maintenance cut, and don't want wash and wear?

The implication here is that you have to look good for *other people*, so here's how to get through it as quickly and painlessly as possible. But what if you want to look good because it makes you *feel* good, not because you're worried about offending the barista at Starbucks with your un-mascaraed eyes? What if it puts you in a better mood, which makes your work and relationships go more smoothly?

There are a couple unspoken assertions going on here:

1. *Stress = bad.*
2. *Everything we do, we do for someone else.* We clean our homes so we won't be mortified when the UPS guy rings. We craft elaborate bento boxes for our kids' lunches because we don't want the other moms to think we're slackers. We work late to impress the boss.

And these assertions raise two questions:

1. Are they true? (*Hell no.*)
2. Isn't there a middle way between zoning out on a mountaintop and being hospitalized with a nervous breakdown? (*Hello, yes*!)

That's what this book is about. You can do everything you want—whether that's to work a job, raise kids, volunteer, have pets, travel, launch non-profits, pursue hobbies, look fabulous, socialize, or enjoy good food and a clean house—all because you *want* to—while only *occasionally* wanting to jab your eyes out with a Sharpie. (Soon, we'll also discuss why this eye-jabbing impulse isn't such a bad thing.) But before we get started, there's a very important mindset adjustment we'll need to make:

Ditch *normal.*

You've probably had this experience: You're standing in a long line for the women's bathroom, and meanwhile the men's bathroom is empty. You know the men's bathroom consists of one room with a lock on the door, so you could potentially go in there and lock the door, and not risk that a dude will walk in on you. But as you eye the 20 women waiting ahead of you, you begin to doubt yourself. If going into the men's room were a good idea, then everyone in line would be doing it, right?

It's the same with anything else. You want to do it all, and you don't want to resign yourself to a life of what-ifs and if-onlys. Maybe you want to work, take care of your family, travel, volunteer, make things happen, shake things up. But the media, some of your friends and relatives, and the general public may think you're nuts, or too ambitious, or an over-achieving snob. Most people don't do all these things, so clearly there's something wrong with even making an attempt to recreate your life to be more full, active, interesting, and fun.

But the problem with popular thinking is that it's often misguided and wrong. The more you choose your actions based on what other people are doing and thinking, the less you'll do what *you* feel is right, and the less fabulously you'll live.

In his book *How Successful People Think*, John C. Maxwell presents this equation: "Popular = Normal = Average."

Do you want to be average? If you're reading this book, probably not. But if you base your thinking on conventional wisdom, average is your fate. Going along with the crowd is definitely easier than thinking for yourself, but it's not the way to live your best life.

We make decisions based on other people's thinking all the time. We automatically send our kids to the same schools our friends and neighbors send their kids to, because that's easier than considering whether our child would be better off in a private school, a charter school, a performing arts school, or even no school. We eat what our families have eaten since childhood, even though we now know, as grown-ups, that it's not good for our bodies. We follow career rules that were set by others years ago, instead of breaking out of the box and trying something different.

If you want to do it all, you're going to have to ditch the *status quo* and go beyond average. *Way* beyond average. That can be scary, because we're built to crave security and routine.

If it helps you overcome the fear of being called crazy, or a snob, or whatever, consider that once you've started to pursue your many goals, you'll be able to inspire and help others do the same. Because secretly, everyone wants to be above average.

So go for it, do it all, ditch average, leave *normal* in the dust—and know that you can be an inspiration to others.

PART 1

The Basics of Doing It All

"Tell me, what is it you plan to do with your one wild and precious life?" —Mary Oliver

You want to do it all. Maybe you want to work a great job, volunteer, socialize, travel, implement crazy new ideas, raise your kids right, be involved in the community, feed yourself and your family well, or keep a sparkling home, all while looking and feeling amazing. I'm right there with you, girl.

But we're misled to believe we can't or shouldn't do it all, even if that's what we really, really want. After all, doing and caring about lots of things can lead to stress. We read articles and blog posts with titles like "Why You Shouldn't Try to Do It All" and "The Dangers of Being Superwoman." It seems pretty clear that being ambitious and action-oriented, and attempting to create a full and memorable life, with the inevitable side effect of stress, is...well, bad.

I disagree heartily. Here in Part 1, we'll talk about how this book can (and can't) help you, what it means to do it all, and some of the reasons we're holding ourselves back.

Chapter 1

What This Book Is (And Isn't)

So: What is this book all about?

It's about living, creating, experiencing, accomplishing, seeing, doing. It's about leaving mediocre behind so you can live a life you'll look back on with pride and happiness, not regret. It's about being active instead of passive, going for awesome instead of average, and being inspired and motivated instead of bored and listless. This book is about ignoring what others think your life can and should be, but also examining your *own* habits and preconceptions, so you can live your very best life.

Ever hear people saying someone "died with their fire still inside them?" This book is about doing the opposite of that.

It's All About Me, Baby

When I showed the D-I-A Manifesto to my friend and business partner Diana, she said something that caused me to change the whole direction of this book: "When I read this as an impartial reader, pretending I didn't know you, I found myself asking, 'What is this woman taking? Because I want some.' I want to know *your* secrets, how *you* do so much."

Originally, this book included a lot of self-help and time management tips that I gleaned from other books and websites, because I wanted to share what had worked for me in my quest to do it all.

But then I realized something: They *didn't* work for me—not as-is, anyway. They *informed* my D-I-A process, but that's it. I integrated bits and pieces from various sources, like coaches, email newsletters, blog posts, podcasts, and self-help books ranging from classic guides to self-published e-books, into a system that works extremely well for the woman who wants to do it all.

After all, everyone who reads a self-help book or blog, or listens to a podcast, or talks to a coach, gets out of it what they need for their situation. A 52-year-old corporate CEO in Chicago gleans different usable advice from books like *Getting Things Done* or *Awaken the Giant Within* than a 29-year-old homeschooling mom in Chattanooga.

Well, when I read/listened to/learned from these sources, I boiled them down to the advice that would work for my goal, which is to live as much and enjoy as much as possible. Many of the techniques became habit, and over time I combined them with new techniques, so now I have a system all my own. A lot of this was done quite unconsciously, so I had to do a lot of thinking about exactly how *I* get it all done.

That's what you'll read in the following pages: The D-I-A strategies and the Plan I synthesized over many years, and how you can use them to create your own fabulous, D-I-A life.

What's Up Next?

I'll talk about the benefits (yes, benefits!) of stress; thought experiments and mind-shifters that will inspire you and help you get over the fear of trying to do it all; and time management and productivity strategies to help you make the time to cram more goodness into your life.

And then there's the D-I-A Plan.

I spoke with women to find out what their most common D-I-A Desires were—what they wished they were doing more of, or what they felt was missing from their lives—and selected the top 12 to create the Plan. I've also included Worksheets that will help you gather the information, resources, and inspiration to make it all happen.

If one of the listed Desires doesn't resonate with you, that's okay. The tactics you'll learn in Part 2 (*The Attitude Adjustment*) and Part 3 (*How to Cram It All In*) can help you with any Desire that isn't listed in the Plan, and I've included a blank Worksheet for you to use for your self-chosen Desire.

You won't be left all on your own to figure out how to make your Plan a reality! Chapter 33, *The Desires*, has one section devoted to each Desire, where I include strategies specific to every one. For example, I offer advice on how to afford travel, how to get started building a business or non-profit, the resources to have on hand to entertain more, and so on.

At the end of the Plan you'll have more travel under your belt, feel and look better, enjoy an uplifting and healthy home environment, be a master at entertaining, volunteer regularly, be more well-read, and more. You'll be active, inspired, and inspirational. You'll learn more than you ever thought possible. And you'll have had loads of great experiences you'll remember forever.

What This Book Is Not

There are also a lot of things this book *is not*, so let's go over them:

This is not a book of motivational platitudes.

My Kindle is full of self-help books that have been only half-read because the entirety of the advice is stuff like:

- Meditate and you'll be happier!
- A gratitude journal will solve all your problems!
- If you can dream it, you can do it!
- Write down your goals on sticky notes and post them all over the house!
- Believe.

Oh wait, I think that last one was from a poster featuring a cat dangling from a tree branch.

I get halfway through the typical personal development book and realize, "Okay, I get it. The big takeaway is *Meditate every day,* and they're going to spend the next 150 pages reiterating why." Or "Ugh! This book is 100 pages explaining why it's so important to say *I love myself* every five minutes."

I'm sure you've seen these tips before, and if they worked for you, you would know it by now and would be doing them. Not only that, but not every technique works for every person, and many of them are ineffective in terms of leading a D-I-A life.

Then there are helpful pieces of advice like "Don't let negative thoughts enter your head" and "Stop feeling guilty over things you can't change," with no follow-up on *how* to make these happen. Like you can just check them off a list: "Don't let negative thoughts enter my head… *check*. Next!"

The advice in this book is different. Yes, I talk about gratitude, values, yoga, and other things you may have heard about before. But my approach to them as a D-I-A practitioner is different than most, and as a former full-time journalist who's written for many health and women's magazines, I understand the value of explaining how to apply my advice in different situations.

This book is not about work-life balance.

Did you get the memo? Work-life balance is a myth. The lines between working and not working have been blurred. Sometimes we need to tap away at the keyboard, or create art, or even answer work calls all night long. Sometimes we check our email during vacation. And sometimes we're sitting in the office on our employer's dime, shopping for new shoes on the Zappos website. So let's not freak out trying to maintain a precise 50/50 split between work and not-work, and worrying that both need to be done in distinct, separate places. Besides, what *is* work? If you run a business you love, or really enjoy your job, does that count as work? My husband enjoys his work so much he *wants* to do it while on vacation.

In any case, if you follow the D-I-A Plan, there will be times when you are decidedly *not* balanced. Depending on the Desire you're working on, you may be spending the lion's share of your time outside the workplace taking classes; refurbishing your home environment; planning trips and traveling; doing fun, amazing stuff with your loved ones; building a side gig; and more. During the Plan, you'll be tackling one new Desire at a time, and that means every so often your balance will shift. And that's okay! You're building a full and exciting life, and that can look a little messy at times.

As long as you're somewhere in the range of normal, you (and your loved ones) will be fine. Your kids and spouse will survive if there are a few weeks where you're not available 24/7. You'll remain employed, even if you have some days where you're not as focused as usual because your mind is spinning with ideas on how to be more well-read, or because all you can think about is the spay/neuter clinic you're volunteering for this weekend. Don't worry if training for your D-I-A Desire *Cross a Finish Line* keeps you from socializing as much as usual, or if you order takeout for a while as you plan a round-the-world trip.

So no, this book is definitely not going to help you with work-life balance.

This book is not about how to make other people happier.

If you're trying to do it all because you're feeling pressure from someone else, whether that's your significant other, your friends, your boss, or society, well, that is not what we mean by *doing it all.* Doing it all is about you. You're the one who will be reviewing your life at the end of each year, and at the end of your life—not your mom, your boss, or the editor of the magazine on your nightstand.

The great news is that if you complete your D-I-A Plan, others are certain to benefit. You'll be an amazing example for your kids. Your family and friends, and the world, will profit more when you're fulfilled, active, and happy, than when you're passive, demotivated, and full of regrets. For example, when you tackle the D-I-A Desire *Volunteer*, you're helping a good cause, and when you work on the D-I-A Desire *Start a Side Hustle*, you're bringing in more cash to support your family, buy gifts for your friends, or donate to your favorite non-profit.

This book is not therapy.

You have low self-esteem, or are depressed, or have an anxiety disorder, or are a perfectionist, procrastinator, or addict. Join the club! While some of the strategies and D-I-A Desires can have the happy outcome of helping alleviate some emotional issues, please don't undertake a D-I-A program as a desperate attempt to fix yourself. Also, if you think you're depressed, if you're having suicidal thoughts, or if some other emotional issue is making your life miserable, I strongly encourage you to see a psychiatrist, therapist, or psychologist right away.

This book is not about beating out the competition, exacting revenge, or making other people jealous.

If you bought this book because you want your best frenemy to weep with envy at your fabulous life, or so you can post your accomplishments on Facebook to show your ex what they're missing out on... please return this book for a refund. *Doing it all* is about *you*, and by extension, it will affect those around you in a positive way by inspiring them and teaching them how they, too, can lead full, purposeful lives.

Don't waste your life trying to do it all just to bring down other people.

Chapter 2

What Does It Mean to Do It All?

Doing it all. Getting it all done. These phrases mean so many things to so many women.

But one key point is that the *all* in doing it all is *things you want to do*. I've said it before, but it's worth saying again:

The *all* is not activities you feel you *should* do. We women have enough *shoulds* in our lives: We *should* have kids, we *should* play nice with rude co-workers, we *should* drive the same safety-conscious car as the other women in our area even though we'd rather tool around in something sleek and cherry red. But your goals need to make your life rich and meaningful and happy, and create memories you'll cherish forever. That's why the goals in the D-I-A plan are called *Desires*.

The *all* is also not things that you want to do because you're afraid people will think you're a loser, a slacker, or just plain weird if you don't. They're not things someone else is telling you to do *or else*.

I've pre-loaded the D-I-A Plan with 12 Desires, but as I mentioned earlier, you can also choose your own, and swap out any that don't resonate with you. In fact, the D-I-A Plan includes a special blank Worksheet just for this reason. Much more on this coming up in Part 4!

Chapter 3

Why We Don't Do It All

Why aren't more of us out there making memories and creating a rewarding life full of fun, purpose, and action? Why are so many of us wasting our precious hours on things that, in the long run, don't matter? Why are we holding back on doing it all in order to please or appease people whose names we won't even remember in five years?

Here are some of the excuses I've heard from women who would love to be doing more…and yet they just can't bring themselves to start.

Excuse #1: *"I'm Not You."*

I find it really interesting when people tell me, "Well, sure, it's easy for *you* to travel. You're self-employed, and have only one kid." Or "It must be nice to be able to get manicures and highlights, and buy nice clothes. But I have a big mortgage, and college tuition to pay for."

Then you get the *think-of-the-children* types who say it's easy for someone to spout off about doing it all when they live in a first world country with running water, where no one is trying to shoot them.

This book is not aimed at dirt-poor populations in war-torn countries. This book is aimed at *you*. If you have the money and time to buy and read this book, you are one of the privileged ones. You are among the richest people on Earth! And if you think the reason you're not doing the things that bring you the most fulfillment is that you have one too many kids, one too few partners, or not exactly the right amount of time or money, then you are fooling yourself.

We all have crap in our lives. Just about everyone who lives a kick-butt D-I-A life has had to make sacrifices, or work through some physical or emotional issue. Last year, the year that inspired this book, I underwent a back surgery that left me in severe pain for months. In Tokyo, I had to jerry-rig a heating pad and an ice pack using gallon-size zip-lock bags, and I had to dope myself up for the flight home because the pain was so intense. Also, because we chose to carry cheap insurance, my husband and I were on the hook for over $20,000 in medical costs. And yet we ran businesses, traveled, and generally had an amazing time.

This book is meant for women, but I have to give you a non-lady example because this dude is pretty darned awesome: Jon Morrow made a fortune in real estate before starting an immensely popular blog called *Boost Blog Traffic*. He lives in a beach house in Mexico, and speaks professionally at events for bloggers and entrepreneurs.

"Well, duh!" you say, "He's single, childless, and loaded."

He also can't move from the neck down.

Jon was born with Spinal Muscular Atrophy, and gradually lost the use of his body. Now, he's one of the oldest people on the planet with his type of SMA.

In a post on *Problogger*, he writes: "I know it's horribly cliché, but if I can quit my job, risk the government carting me off to a nursing home because I can't afford my own healthcare, convince my poor mother to abandon her career and drive my crippled butt 3,000 miles to a foreign country, and then make enough money to support myself, my mother, my father, and an entire nursing staff using nothing but my voice, then what can you accomplish if you really set your mind to it?"

We all have problems, but we also have superpowers. To throw up your hands and give up on your dreams because the universe hasn't lined up events exactly the way you feel they must be in order for you to have a go at it—I call BS. It's an excuse.

When you see someone doing all the things you want to do, don't pick apart their lives to figure out what makes them so different from you that they can do these things and you can't. Use them as inspiration, and figure out how you can make it happen for you, as well.

Excuse #2: *"I Really Don't Have Time for All This!"*

In my brief stint as a wellness coach, almost every one of my clients said they didn't have the time to exercise, or prepare healthy meals, or meditate, or practice self-care, but later revealed that they watched TV for at least an hour each night.

If I pointed out that everyone was busy, they'd say, "Yes, but I'm *really* busy. I work two jobs, I have four kids, I volunteer at my church, I take care of my ailing parents. I *literally* have no time."

Here's something to consider: The people who are getting important things done, who are running marathons, writing novels, launching businesses, starting non-profits, traveling the world, and digging wells in Africa aren't some lucky breed of folk who are less busy, or magically have more time than everyone else. They don't have maids, they usually have families, and they often have full-time jobs.

They just make better use of their time.

Instead of sleeping in, they train. Instead of watching TV, they study. They understand the premise of Laura Vanderkam's wonderful book *168 Hours: You Have More Time Than You Think*, which is that, well, we all have 168 hours in a week. Even if you work eight hours a day, five days per week, and sleep eight hours a night, that still leaves you 72 hours every week. And time-use studies show that people work less and spend less time on chores and child care than they think, so those tasks are no excuse.

Figure out what's sucking up all your free time. Facebook? TV? Errands? Shopping? Eating? Talking on the phone? Worrying? Then ask yourself: "How can I better use that time to get done all the important things I want to accomplish this year?"

Somewhere in those 72 hours per week outside of work and sleep, you should be able to find the time to go after your D-I-A Desires. In Part 3, *How to Cram It All In*, we'll talk about some surprising, counter-intuitive strategies to do just that.

Excuse #3: *"I'm So Not Motivated."*

This is a biggie. You say you want to do it all, but when the time comes to walk your talk, you suddenly…just don't feel like it. Boy, does that sofa look good right now!

Trust me, everyone feels this way sometimes. Some people feel this way all the time! Here's what works for me when I drop into that lethargic, uninspired state:

Act first, get motivated later.

A few years ago, I noticed a friend of mine had a photocopied excerpt of Julie Fast's book *Get It Done When You're Depressed* on her refrigerator. I was so impressed with the excerpt that I bought and read the book, and then interviewed Julie for the *Renegade Writer* blog.

One of her points that stuck with me is that you can't wait to feel motivated or inspired *before* you do something, because if you're depressed, you'll *never* feel motivated. You'll just wait and wait to feel that spark of inspiration, and it won't happen.

Even if we're not clinically depressed, we often sit around and gaze at our navels and try to figure out why we're not motivated to go after our D-I-A Desires, and what we can do about it. We think and analyze and ponder…and never leave our chairs to take action. The shocking news is that you simply can't think your way into being motivated, no matter how much you try, and no matter how many motivational books you read and rah-rah podcasts you listen to.

If you're lolling around on the couch, waiting for motivation to hit before you get up and train for the 5k you signed up for, you'll be on that couch so long that it will have a permanent you-shaped imprint on it. Getting started *despite the fact that you feel uninspired* will generate the motivation to keep going. Once you're doing the task, you'll often feel compelled to keep going and do even more.

Lack of motivation is an excuse—even though it may be unconscious—whose goal is to protect you from becoming uncomfortable or embarrassed. See it for what it is, and rock on with your D-I-A life.

Excuse #4: *"I Don't Have the Money."*

If you were able to buy this book, and have a stable place to live, an internet connection, and food in the pantry, then I'm not buying your cries of poverty.

Remember that list of things my family and I did, saw, created, and accomplished in 2015? We're a solidly middle-class family…I even used an online income calculator to be sure. My husband and I both work for a living; we didn't win the lottery, and we didn't inherit gobs of cash. In the D-I-A Plan we'll discuss tactics that will help you make your D-I-A Desires a reality, even if you're like me—a typical working woman who is decidedly not rolling in cash.

If you want it, you'll *find a way.*

One time I was complaining to a writing coach that I wasn't charging as much as I needed to for certain writing products, but I was afraid that if I raised the prices, people wouldn't be able to afford them. After all, you've heard of the starving writer trope, right? My coach replied with something that has changed my entire attitude about what people can or cannot afford: "Other people's finances are none of your business."

In other words, if someone really wants something, they'll find a way to get it, and how they do it is none of your concern. They may dip into their nest egg, barter, use a credit card, or borrow the money from a friend or family member. And that's fine, because what I'm offering has enough value to the customer that they'll do what it takes to get their hands on it.

I have a friend who's been saying for years that she wants to start a gift shop, but when I ask her why she doesn't just do it already, she says she doesn't have the money. Do you think all the people who own the stores lining Main Street had a million dollars lying around, and just pulled a big wad of money out of their pocket to start their businesses? No: They most likely got a loan from the bank or begged their friends and relatives to invest, or maybe they Kickstarted that business. They took a great financial risk because it was something they really wanted. I'm sure my friend knows all this, but *I don't have the money* is a socially acceptable excuse that generally gets people to shut up.

So if you want to do it all, but are moaning about the state of your bank account:

Hack your travel. Rent-A-Wreck. Unschool your kids. Barter your services. Trade a product. Dip into your savings. Couch surf. Borrow from the library. Borrow from a friend. Shop on Craigslist. Bootstrap. Freecycle. Design on a dime. Hire a high-schooler. Rent out your guest room. Get a loan. Sell something. Fly standby. Housesit. Hold a fundraiser. Kickstart your business. Host cheap movie nights. Open a gift registry.

It's all about priorities.

I'll bet you've had this experience: You ask a friend to go see that new blockbuster movie with you, and she says she can't afford it. But a week later, she rolls up in a brand new Mercedes and starts bragging about her ski trip. What's that all about?

It's because what people can afford is entirely subjective. Often when someone says they can't afford something, what they mean is that it's not a priority for them. Your friend wasn't as interested in seeing the new *Star Wars* movie as she was in buying a new car and going on a ski trip.

Is doing it all a priority for you? Traveling, starting a side business, volunteering, keeping a pleasant home, competing, learning—are these really priorities? If so, it's key to figure out where your money is being spent on non-priorities, and divert it to the important things.

We often spend money on trivialities because we're simply used to having that cash sucked out of our bank account, and it's easier to let it keep happening than to upset the *status quo*. I recommend going over every expense and figuring out which ones you can cut.

For example, a couple years ago I went on a savings spree and saved $40 per month by choosing a new phone plan with less data based on our usage, and $30 per month by decreasing the data plan on my iPad. That doesn't sound like a lot, but it's equal to two sessions with a personal trainer where I live! I then cut our home and auto insurance costs by $700 per year, and sliced our food bills in half. Not to mention we moved from New Hampshire to North Carolina, in part to save enough that I could work less and do more other stuff—and thanks to that move we're saving over *$18,000 per year* in mortgage, heating bills, health insurance, and child care.

It's not as expensive as you think.

You can start a business with a free WordPress website. Volunteering is free...and so is training for a marathon...and so is keeping your house spotless...and so is writing a book. If you're working on the

D-I-A Desire *Entertain*, throw pot-luck parties or invite friends over to watch movies and nosh on popcorn. If *Cross a Finish Line* is your current D-I-A Desire, join a free community-based running club. Heck, you don't even need fancy running shoes. An article on *Outside Magazine's* website says: "Your time is better spent crafting the right balance between mileage and intensity, on eating and sleeping well, on strength training and mental toughness. There's simply not much evidence that you need to worry about shoes."

You *can* do it all, no matter how much money you have in the bank.

Excuse #5: *"I Don't Want to Be Different."*

I agree: Doing it all is definitely not normal, and you'll probably hear as much from well-meaning friends, relatives, and co-workers.

However, the normal person—at least here in the US—is unhealthy, working a job they don't love, and rushing from one unimportant task to another until they fall into bed, exhausted...so they can do it all over again the next day.

The Nielsen media rating company reports that the average person in America watches five hours of TV every day, according to the *New York Daily News*. On top of that, the article says: "The average American then spends another 32 minutes a day on time-shifted television, an hour using the internet on a computer, an hour and seven minutes on a smartphone, and two hours, 46 minutes listening to the radio."

Then the normal American complains that they don't have the time or energy to pursue their passions and do it all.

Are you still sure you want to be normal?

I love this quote from Louise Hay's book *You Can Heal Your Soul*: "We are meant to be different. When we can accept this, then there is no competition and no comparison. To try to be like another is to shrivel our soul."

Excuse #6: *"I Don't Want to Be a Bitch!"*

Depending on what our D-I-A life looks like, we get various names thrown at us:

- Superwoman. (Which doesn't sound so bad, except it's usually said with a sneer.)
- Type-A.
- Anal-retentive.
- OCD.
- Bitch, or its variants Bitch on wheels and Bitch on steroids.
- Tiger mom.
- The Energizer Bunny.

Who wants to be called a bitch because she cares about the state of her home environment, or anal-retentive because she has standards for how she looks, or Type-A because she produces four amazing blog posts per week and volunteers for three organizations while raising six kids? I'm sure you can see how this cultural narrative surrounding ambitious women keeps a lot of us from even trying.

Ever see a grammar police-type person post a comment on someone's blog, or in an Amazon review, picking out the three typos they were horrified to find in the author's work? And then the author's supporters jump in saying, "Yeah, well, at least she wrote a book. What have *you* done?"

That's the attitude we need here. "Yeah, maybe I come off as a superwoman wannabe because I had the house spring cleaned while launching a business and learning Swahili, but what have *you* done lately? At least no one will call you a Type-A bitch, if that's any consolation."

Excuse #7: *"It's Selfish!"*

You're leading this great life doing everything you dream of, living your vision, achieving your goals, and accumulating a huge list of accomplishments. And some of your friends are saying pointedly, "I wish *I* had time to pursue a hobby," and your co-workers are sniping, "Must be nice to have the money to host parties and go on trips."

Then you feel like it's somehow *wrong* to pursue all the things you want to do, accomplish, create, learn, and experience. As if your success is stealing pleasure and success from the people you love.

It's *them*, not you.

Doing it all is not a zero-sum game. Your D-I-A Plan does not keep a single other person on Earth from pursuing the same path. In fact, when you're happy and fulfilled, you're in a better position to help others by inspiring them to action and helping them along the way.

Excuse #8: *"I Feel Guilty."*

We can do it all, but we can't do it all at once. There's an opportunity cost to everything we do: If we're working out at the gym to prep for a race, we're not reading to our kids. If we're reading to our kids, we're not working on our non-profit. If we're writing a grant application for our non-profit, then we're not writing our novel. If we're writing our novel, we're not planning a trip. You get the idea.

And because we can't do it all at once, we feel guilty. For many of us, not doing something at any given moment equates to *neglecting* that thing. No matter that while we're at the gym, our kids are happily playing Candyland with the babysitter at home. It doesn't register with us that if we stop writing our novel for a while to work on a grant application, the novel will still be there waiting for us when we're done. We feel we're procrastinating on the trip planning when we're writing our novel, even though there will be plenty of time to make a packing list when we've wrapped up the chapter we're sweating over right now.

In the D-I-A Plan in this book, you'll find you can get it all done at the time that's right for every goal, so you can ditch the guilt for good.

Excuse #9: *"You Call That Spiritual?"*

"But…but…my life coach told me I should stop striving and try to cultivate a sense of ease, and my yoga instructor says we shouldn't attach to outcomes!"

Your life coach, yoga instructor, spiritual guide, whatever—they're all right.

I've been practicing yoga and meditation since 1997, and am very aware that the D-I-A concept seems to directly conflict with the concepts of surrender, non-attachment, and acceptance of the present moment. After all, by doing it all, we're trying to change *what is*, right?

We're showing the universe we're not perfectly contented with our lot. That's bad, isn't it?

It depends.

There's been a cultural shift for women (at least if the women's mags are any indication) toward all things Zen—accepting what is, being happy no matter what the circumstances, expressing gratitude for our blessings, and greeting irritating people and situations with a compassionate smile. The phrase *It is what it is* has invaded the vernacular.

That's wonderful. There are many things we can't control, and it makes sense to accept them, rather than rail against what we can't change. Sometimes it rains on your birthday. Sometimes the company you work for goes belly-up and you're out of a job.

But in some cases, we put on our Zen faces for things we can and should change, because we're feeling under-confident about taking charge. We're afraid that we'll upset other people if we insist on doing what we want, even if we're perfectly justified in doing so, or we're feeling lazy or unmotivated, and it's just easier to pretend to accept the way things are. The whole Zen thing? In cases like these, it's an excuse.

Accepting *what is* can sometimes translate into settling for less than you deserve, or making do with less than you need, and it can lead to you *not* going after a big, D-I-A life. When you settle or make do, you're giving up and letting the situation control you. You're saying other people or your environment are in charge of you, and you're going to just roll over and learn to deal with it. The philosophy of accepting *what is*, when used at the wrong times, keeps you from making the changes you really want and need in your life.

The phrase *It is what it is* often means *Shut up and deal with it*. If you say, "I wish I could travel more" and your sister replies, "It is what it is," I don't think she's a Zen master. I think she's just trying to get you to shut up about it.

Take It Easy

So is there a way to go after our D-I-A Desires with a sense of motivation and drive, and still maintain a sense of peace, acceptance, and ease so we can bust this excuse for good?

By *maintaining peace*, I'm not talking about shunning stress, as we will discuss in Chapter 4, *Say Yes to Stress*, but about keeping sight of the real reason we're doing it all: Because we love it and it gives us joy, even if we give our all to something and it goes sideways.

Go after your D-I-A Desires, but don't be married to specific results. Hope, but don't require. You may take action and do all the right things, but the outcome may not look exactly like you envisioned—and that's okay. So you don't avoid writing a novel because you think you suck as a writer, and then tell yourself *It is what it is*. You spend six months writing a novel, knowing that it might suck, but you can live with that. Because now you've finished it!

You might train for your half marathon and be flattened by the flu the day of the event. You could work hard to create the perfect space in your home to rest and relax in, and when the paint dries you realize the color reminds you of the geriatric wing at the hospital. You could spend weeks planning a trip to Disney World with your kids, and then your flight is cancelled, or it rains all day every day, or one of the kids gets sick and you lose your table at the Crystal Palace.

Remember, you can still look back with happiness and pride on these attempts—and even failing beats out watching TV, surfing the web, eating mindlessly, and beating yourself up for never trying. Better to say "I tried and failed and moved on" than "I never tried because I thought I might fail."

Even if the outcome isn't what you were hoping for, you still have that novel draft (which can be rewritten!) and the improvements in your writing that came from all that practice; you have better stamina and improved strength from running; walls can be repainted; you have hilarious photos of your kids standing drenched in front of the Cinderella Castle.

Later in this book, when you're working on your D-I-A Plan, keep in mind that you're doing it all to create a life full of worthwhile activities and fun—and that can manifest in unexpected ways.

PART 2
The Attitude Adjustment

"Life is not a dress rehearsal." —Rose Tremain

So we've established that you want to go after all the goals you've set as Desires in your life, whether those be to work, play, have kids, keep pets, volunteer, travel, or entertain...all while feeling and looking incredible and enjoying your beautiful home.

A D-I-A Plan requires you to be self-motivated...inspired...a go-getter. It also requires that you not let fear, distraction, low motivation, or a lack of belief in yourself get in the way of your D-I-A Desires. So in Part 2, we'll work on creating the mental energy and positive habits you'll need to make it through the next amazing phase of your life.

The internet, books, and magazines are overflowing with tips meant to get you motivated and inspired. If you've found techniques that work for you, please use them. But here, I'll describe the strategies I've synthesized from years of experience and experimentation that have helped me—and can help you—do it all.

Now...let's get motivated!

Chapter 4

Say Yes to Stress

In the opening to this book you read about my 2015 and all the crazy and stressful, but fun and memorable things I planned and accomplished.

My desire to do it all it goes back much further than 2015. In high school, I studied so many languages that I didn't have a lunch period or a study hall, and was already submitting short stories to literary journals. In college and graduate school, I took almost double the normal course load while also working and volunteering, and maintained an A- grade point average. And it goes on from there.

I *could* cut down on my activities and spend my days reading light novels, soaking in lavender-infused baths, and om-ing away on a yoga mat. And the people and things in my life would get along just fine. After all, no one's family died because their window shades were dusty. The world won't stop spinning if I don't read voraciously, start social clubs, volunteer, adopt special-needs pets, host teenage exchange students, or run multiple businesses.

And yet I've constantly put myself in situations where I knew I'd be exhausted before it was all over. I've teamed up with a friend to sew 80 cat beds for the local shelter. And planned multi-country trips with a 6-year-old. And started clubs and organizations where I ended up managing 100 or more members or volunteers. And agreed to write 13 magazine articles in a month. And attempted to run two businesses while homeschooling our son. And had two bathrooms renovated during the Christmas holiday, while hosting three additional holiday dinners for people who couldn't be there for the main one. Of course, while I did all this, it was important that my teeth were flossed daily, my hair was highlighted every six weeks, and all my bras were hand-washed on a regular basis.

But Should We Flee Stress?

So yes, I've always experienced that major, scary problem women's magazines and books and blogs try so kindly to help us avoid—stress. I journal, take hot baths, and get frequent massages, and I'm very involved in yoga and meditation. But when you get up from *savasana* and jump back into 20 crazy projects at once, the pressure is sure to come back before you can say *Namaste*.

Stress can feel like crap. But is it really something to be avoided at all costs?

As I was writing this chapter, I received a newsletter from author Laura Vanderkam titled *The Good Life Is Not Always the Easy Life*, and it perfectly encapsulates my thoughts on the subject. Laura gave me permission to quote from it here:

> *[...]no one is entitled to a stress-free life, and shying from stress can cut off much happiness.*
>
> *Here's what I mean. In life, there's effortless fun and effortful fun. Cracking open a beer and turning on the TV after the kids go to bed falls in the first category. Planning a dinner party falls in the second. Both have their place, but it's always easy to underinvest in the latter because, well, it's work. The idea that fun should take work is incongruous enough that we resist it. Most of us are busy enough with professional work and family work that turning leisure time into work just sounds ridiculous. Better not to make a fuss.*
>
> *That's fine except that watching TV for the bulk of one's leisure time does not make for a particularly meaningful or memorable life. When I think about the things that I would mention as highlights of my leisure time over the last year, they're almost all effortful. Running 3 half-marathons was great in retrospect, but there were many not-fun moments of finding parking and waiting in the heat or cold for the start. Baking with my 4-year-old is mar-*

velous in many ways, but it is never easy with her toddler brother underfoot. I loved bringing my daughter to eat with the princesses at Epcot's Akershus in September. Hauling the kids around hot, crowded Disney World, on the other hand, which was necessary in order to eat with those princesses, was at times horrific enough to be comical.

[...]I think that being able to "hold paradox" can be useful in all realms of life. Rather than say "I want to have fun and this is not fun," those who can hold paradox think this: Often fun takes work. This is simply its nature, much as the human body must eat and sleep to function. There is no such thing as a stress-free life, and there is no point wishing that fun will just come to you. If you want joyful communities, marvelous vacations, and fun family activities, you can create them. You can know that there will be a lot of bother and some horrible moments. You can also know that there will be good moments, memorable moments, and most importantly, moments that would not have happened had you chosen to save your energy, skip the bother, and do nothing instead.

Who looks back with pride at the end of the year (or at the end of their lives) on how much TV they watched, or how many Facebook posts they commented on? Most likely, every moment in your life you remember with fondness and pride took effort...and effort often means stress.

Not All Stress is Bad

The women's media helpfully remind us—pretty much non-stop—that stress can cause every medical woe that plagues humankind, from heart disease to cancer.

And that is true, *if* you're talking about constant, oppressive, chronic stress, like when you're caring for a spouse with dementia or living in a refugee camp. But the stress you'll experience in doing your D-I-A Plan is the acute kind of stress you feel when, say, planning a wedding, prepping for an important exam, giving a speech, interviewing for the job of your dreams, or standing at the starting line of a marathon. Acute stress ramps up in response to a particular stressor, and it can actually help you perform better...and then it ramps back down during and after the anxiety-provoking event.

Many of us say we work better under a looming deadline. Henry Fonda threw up from anxiety before every stage performance, even at the age of 75. And in my book *Commit: How to Blast Through Problems & Reach Your Goals Through Massive Action*, I talk about how much more effective it is to set big goals, like committing to make 50 sales calls in a day rather than five, because the hit of acute stress you feel from the bigger number will motivate you and improve your performance.

Here's proof from the American Psychological Association website that the right kind of stress can lead to a happier life: "Myth: Stress is always bad for you. According to this view, zero stress makes us happy and healthy. Wrong. Stress is to the human condition what tension is to the violin string: Too little and the music is dull and raspy; too much and the music is shrill or the string snaps. Stress can be the kiss of death or the spice of life. The issue, really, is how to manage it. Managed stress makes us productive and happy; mismanaged stress hurts and even kills us."

Adding to that, a study published in the *Psychological Bulletin* concluded: "Stressors with the temporal parameters of the fight-or-flight situations faced by humans' evolutionary ancestors elicited potentially beneficial changes in the immune system. The more a stressor deviated from those parameters by becoming more chronic, however, the more components of the immune system were affected in a potentially detrimental way." In plain English, the temporary bump in stress caused by planning a trip, writing a novel, or starting a side business won't kill you—and will, in fact, make you stronger.

A certain amount of physical stress is actually *good* for you. Take weightlifting, where you're stressing and creating micro-tears in muscle fibers; the repair process is what makes your muscles grow. We're also starting to see that intermittent fasting can help us safely lose weight, and maybe even live longer.

However, if the stress of doing it all is keeping you from actually *enjoying* your life, something has to change. Sure, it's nice to look back on 200 amazing things you accomplished last year, but not if you also recall that during every one of those 365 days you snapped at your kids, yelled at your spouse, complained to your friends, and locked yourself in the bathroom at 9 pm with a glass of pinot noir because you *just can't anymore.*

Everyone has those times where they've just had it. For example, I'm writing this chapter from a hotel 15 minutes from my house because after the holidays—three full weeks with guests, home renovations, entertaining, a 6-year-old and an exchange student needing entertainment and rides, and me trying just to *get some freaking work done*—I was ready to aim a Sharpie toward my eyeballs.

But on a day-to-day basis, I'm a very happy person. I love my life, and I'm grateful for all of it. I enjoy what I do, and if I don't, I find some way to delegate it or delete it.

The point of doing it all is that you love all the things you're doing, and you don't want to say no to any of them, and they somehow fulfill your personal values. If you're trying to do it all and it makes you feel cranky, resentful, or just plain unhappy on a continuous basis, that's not even close to the *doing it all* we're talking about here.

So I say bring on the stress, if that's what it takes to create meaning and lasting memories. And when the pressure gets to be too much, find ways to mitigate it so you can get back to doing everything you want.

Chapter 5

Give Your Values Center Stage

Why are you putting yourself through the stress of doing it all? After all, a D-I-A Plan can be uncomfortable. Sometimes it's worse than uncomfortable. You may need to change your attitude toward hard work, give up some well-worn habits, and withstand snarky comments from friends and co-workers. Why bother?

In order for the D-I-A Plan to make sense, and be worth the effort, it needs to connect to your deepest values. In wellness coaching, we're taught to help clients figure out the higher purpose behind their goals—a purpose so important and right that it makes them truly want to work until they realize their dream. If you're working for the right reason, you'll feel all fired up, and nothing will keep you from reaching your D-I-A Desires.

What Floats Your Boat?

Look up *personal values* online and you'll find plenty of highly involved, multi-step instructions on identifying your values. But I don't think it needs to be that complicated; you probably have an idea of what's important to you already.

Some examples of personal values include:

- Abundance
- Achievement
- Balance
- Comfort

- Creativity
- Faith
- Honesty
- Hospitality
- Intensity
- Intimacy
- Joy
- Loyalty
- Mastery
- Nature
- Outrageousness
- Poise
- Popularity
- Respect
- Self-control
- Sexiness
- Wealth
- Wisdom

When you get to the D-I-A Plan in Part 4, I'll be asking you to choose your top personal values from the bonus downloadable Values Checklist, and then determine how each of the D-I-A Desires helps you meet these values. But please keep this information in the back of your mind as you read this chapter, and the rest of the book, so you have a chance to process and absorb it. This forethought can help you when you're ready to tackle that part of your D-I-A Plan.

For example, let's say one of your highest values is learning and education. How can you connect that with the D-I-A Desire *Travel*? Here are some thoughts:

- There's no better way to learn about other cultures than by traveling. You can try to learn from a book or the internet, but actually being in that place and talking to the people who live there will give you much greater insights.
- Depending on where you go, you may need to learn at least a few phrases in a foreign language. When our son helped my

husband out at a trade show in Tokyo, he had to learn to say "hello" and "thank you" in Japanese.

- Going on a camping trip will teach you and your family more about nature.
- Before you go on any trip, you can buy or borrow a guidebook to the area, or use Wikipedia, to glean facts about the population, landmarks, major exports, monetary units, and so on.
- If you bring your kids on trips, they'll learn more about the world. My son's school allows time off for trips because they consider traveling educational.
- Even a day trip to a nearby city or state can be very educational. We've learned a lot from walking the Freedom Trail in Boston, going to the Library of Congress and the Smithsonian Air & Space Museum in Washington, DC, and even touring a battleship in our current home state of North Carolina.

Or maybe one of your core values is love and connection. How does *that* connect with the D-I-A Desire of *Travel*? Here are several ideas:

- If you travel with your family or friends, you get to spend time with your loved ones doing something fun. Nothing connects people like having new experiences together and struggling through the hard times that sometimes come with travel—like long plane rides, language barriers, and weird toilets.
- You can travel to visit friends in other states and countries. We recently visited a friend in Belgium whom we hadn't seen in 20 years.
- When you travel, you learn to appreciate other cultures and viewpoints, which makes you a more compassionate person.
- You could show your love for others by going on a volunteer vacation.

You get the idea: You're boosting your motivation by connecting each D-I-A Desire with your most deeply held values. And if one of the Desires simply doesn't match up with any of your values, you can swap it out for a different Desire that does. That's what the blank Worksheet is for!

Your mind isn't stupid, and it has an amazing BS detector. If you want it to go along with the hard work and occasional stress of following a D-I-A Plan, it needs a darned good reason.

In Chapter 33 you'll be learning about the 12 D-I-A Desires, and for each Desire, just to get your idea machine going, I offer examples of how it can fulfill various randomly-chosen personal values. In the meantime, start contemplating: What are *your* core values?

Chapter 6

Fight the Resistance

A lot of the time, it's not that we don't want to do something, but when we're about to start, we feel a sense of internal refusal that's almost *physical.*

In his book *The War of Art,* Stephen Pressfield calls this feeling Resistance, and he writes, "The more important a call or action is to our soul's evolution, the more Resistance we will feel toward pursuing it." In the book, Resistance shows up in many forms, from substance abuse to despair, but here we'll focus on that powerful sense of negative energy we feel when we're about to start something new. Pressfield says that some of the activities that most commonly elicit Resistance include:

- Any creative art, such as writing, painting, or dance.
- Launching a business, non-profit, or any other enterprise.
- Improving your diet or health habits.
- Attempts at spiritual advancement.
- Education of any kind.
- Acts that require moral or ethical courage, or that will help others.

These sound a lot like the D-I-A Desires! The more important the goal is to you, and the more likely it is the goal will improve you or your life, the stronger the Resistance is.

Resistance is what makes you dredge up even the most unlikely excuse for not following your Plan, and what makes that excuse seem perfectly reasonable. You have no time! You're not good enough! You have no money! People will laugh at you! It's a selfish goal! But as Pressfield says, "Resistance is always lying and always full of shit."

You really want to do it all. You're on the verge of working your Plan. But some unseen force within you screams, "Stop, this is dangerous!" What do you do? Here are a few strategies that can help short-term when you're feeling stuck.

Time It

One way to get yourself started in spite of Resistance is to set a timer for ten minutes, and promise yourself that if you feel like stopping when the timer goes off, you can. Usually, once you get past the stuck feeling, you'll create a momentum that keeps you going. For example, if you don't feel inspired to work on your writing project, tell yourself that all you have to do is open a word processing file and write for ten minutes. Getting those first words down is the hardest part, but once you've broken through that Resistance, chances are you won't want to stop.

Create a Values Board

Many women have a vision board, but for me a values board works better. What's the difference? A vision board has images of what you want from your life; for example, you may pin up photos of places you want to visit, the giant house you wish you had, and a big wad of cash. But a values board boasts images of *why* you're going after a D-I-A Plan, and reminds you of what all this hard work is for.

My top values are freedom, health, fun, and family, so in my office I have a bulletin board on which I've created a collage of photos and images related to these values: A stock-art photo of fruits and berries, a photo of my son at a ballet demo, a clip-art image of a plane flying over landmarks like the Eiffel Tower and the Statue of Liberty, and more.

When I'm feeling all *Man, I don't want to do X today*, I look at the board and am hit with a sense of urgency to do something that fulfills these values. This gives me a jolt of motivation that powers me through my tasks.

Test this tactic yourself, but don't overanalyze and turn your values board project into another form of procrastination. You already know what your values are from Chapter 5, *Give Your Values Center Stage*. Quickly scan your cache of photos, pages of old magazines, and free online image galleries to find pictures that embody your values, and pin them up on a bulletin board or right on your wall. When Resistance hits, take a look at your board, and you'll be reminded why your D-I-A Plan is so important to you.

Get Into the Right Box

Take a piece of paper and draw two lines to divide it into four quadrants. Label the upper left quadrant *Urgent, Not Important*. The upper right is *Urgent and Important*. Label the lower left quadrant *Not Urgent, Not Important*, and the lower right, *Not Urgent, Important*.

See the upper and lower left quadrants? Those boxes are where Resistance wants you to stay. When you feel that strong sense of negative energy about calling the volunteer organizer, writing a memoir, breaking out the language-learning app, or studying for your certification, the tasks in those two boxes suddenly seem crucial to your survival. "Those baseboards are looking grimy, and I simply cannot work on my new business until they're sparkling. And I just remembered the cats need brushing, too." Even the upper right quadrant, tasks that are *Urgent and Important*, get in on the game.

Most of the tasks for your D-I-A Plan lie in the lower right: They're not urgent, but they are important. They may not be fires that need to be put out right now, but they are key to you thriving and leading a full life.

If you don't want to draw your own quadrants, download any one of hundreds online. Fill in the tasks for the day (or week, or month) according to their urgency and importance. When you're about to get started on something on your D-I-A Plan, cover each quadrant except the lower right and pretend they don't exist, so you can focus on going after your Desires without any distraction.

Maybe you can't permanently beat Resistance, but you can definitely trick it long enough to get some major work done toward your D-I-A Desires.

Chapter 7
Do Actual Work

I recently read a blog post by one of my favorite business coaches, Naomi Dunford of Ittybiz, on the value of working really hard and what that looks like. This concept of working hard immediately resonated with me as a mentor for writers. I'm always getting emails from writers who tell me they're having trouble making it work, even though they're trying really, super hard. But when I ask them what they actually did this week toward building their writing business, they draw a blank.

Many of us don't give 100% to our goals. We give maybe 50 to 70%, tops. We say we're working hard, but our definition of hard work is a loose one. So as you're pursuing your D-I-A Desires, I want you to think about this: Naomi pointed out that you're only working hard in the moment when you are *physically working*—taking physical actions that someone looking at you would be able to recognize as working hard.

You're not trying hard when you *think* about working on a D-I-A Desire, or *worry* about it, or *contemplate* it, or *plan it* to death. If you were to watch someone on a screen when they're working hard, you would know that's what they're doing. There would be visual clues that would make you say, "Wow, they're really working hard." If you saw them thinking or planning or contemplating, it would look like they were doing nothing.

For example, if you're working on the Desire *Cross a Finish Line*, working hard might look like you being on the local track, or at the gym, sweating through the miles. If, for the Desire *Start a Side Hustle*, you want to start a dog-walking business, working hard means an outside observer would see you posting flyers, building your website, and calling pet stores, veterinary clinics, and dog groomers to drum up leads. For the D-I-A Desire *Become Well-Read*, working hard would look like you actually reading books or magazines, not obsessively scrolling through Goodreads reviews looking for books to borrow, or buying a stack of magazines that you then walk by with a guilty feeling ten times per day.

Writers fall prey to this trap big-time (and *Write* is one of the D-I-A Desires, so this is relevant to you!). Working hard at your writing doesn't mean reading books about writing, or taking courses on writing, or planning your writing schedule for next week, or going to therapy to rid you of your deep-seated fear of rejection. It means doing those activities that will result in a completed work of writing (putting words on a page), and doing your very best at them.

How many of us really try our very best at anything? How many of us truly work hard? Sure, we *say* we're working hard, but that's because we're expending so much mental effort in doing everything *but* the thing that will get results, it feels like hard work. It exhausts our brains!

But the only way to get actual results in your D-I-A Plan is to *do actual work.*

Adopt a Mantra

I've adopted the mantra *Work hard.* Not just for my business, but in every aspect of my life where I want to accomplish something measurable.

When I'm working out I tell myself, "Work hard!" When I pass a kitchen counter that's piled with dishes destined for the dishwasher and am tempted to just keep walking, I think, "Work hard!" As I'm critiquing ideas and queries in the forums of a writing class, and am ready to throw in the towel before the work is done, I remind myself, "Work hard!"

I find that with this mantra, I can eke out a few more reps, I can keep my house and life in order, and *I can get a lot of stuff done.*

What if you adopted this mantra for yourself? Or use one like:

- "Always do your best."
- "Could I be doing something better right now?"
- "What would it look like if I were working really hard right now?"

Test it out for yourself, and see if your productivity improves.

What Does Working Hard Look Like to You?

It may be difficult to recognize what trying hard looks like, since we're so used to creating mental smoke and calling it work. So as part of the Worksheet for each D-I-A Desire, I'll ask you to brainstorm what it would look like if you were trying your best at accomplishing that Desire. That way, you won't be fooled into spinning your wheels and calling it a day.

Chapter 8

Inconsistency Is A-OK

Here's a quote I strive to live by: "A foolish consistency is the hobgoblin of little minds, adored by little statesmen and philosophers and divines. With consistency a great soul has simply nothing to do. He may as well concern himself with his shadow on the wall. Speak what you think now in hard words, and to-morrow speak what to-morrow thinks in hard words again, though it contradict every thing you said to-day. — 'Ah, so you shall be sure to be misunderstood.' — Is it so bad, then, to be misunderstood? Pythagoras was misunderstood, and Socrates, and Jesus, and Luther, and Copernicus, and Galileo, and Newton, and every pure and wise spirit that ever took flesh. To be great is to be misunderstood." —Ralph Waldo Emerson

Occasionally I get emails from readers saying things like, "In this blog post you said you get up at 5 am, but then in today's email you mentioned sleeping in until nine. What's up with that?"

To which I reply, "I wrote that blog post three months ago, and at that time I *was* getting up at 5 am. It worked for me then, but it's not working for me right now."

I have loads of tips in this book that can help you kick D-I-A butt, but I don't want you to think you have to use all of them, all the time. You're smart, and I know you can figure out which time management and attitude adjustment tips will work for you, and at what times. You may start a Naikan practice (see Chapter 16, *Practice Extreme Gratitude*), and after a month you stop because it no longer interests you. This is a sign that you may not need this technique right now, or that it isn't working for you at this moment. After all, if you felt marvelous and empowered every time you did something, would you really stop? Even if you do stop now, you may find yourself drawn to it again in the future. Situations change. People change.

Also, you often need to experiment to know what works best for you. Your best gal pal may swear by her morning routine, but if you're an inveterate night owl and love staying up into the wee hours, it may not work for you. I always recommend trying every tactic out just to be sure, but don't think that just because you attempt something, you have to do it forever. Why keep using a D-I-A tactic you don't enjoy, or that doesn't work for you?

So don't worry that you'll come off as a hypocrite for singing the praises of meditation, and then falling off the om-wagon for a few months. Meditation does work for many people, much of the time, and for that reason you praise it. But you don't have to stick with any tactic beyond the point of usefulness just to appear consistent to other people.

Chapter 9

Die Before You Die

We're all faced with decisions almost every minute of the day. Should I have oatmeal for breakfast or a smoothie? Should I wear the black boots or the brown? Should we go to the museum or the park? We make most of these decisions quickly and easily.

Sometimes, though, the decisions we make aren't so much *easy* as *unconscious*. It's almost natural for us to put off planning a trip because the logistics are so complicated, say no to volunteering because we don't have the time, decline invitations in order to squeeze in a few more episodes of that Netflix sensation, let our homes become seedy because we're too tired to clean up, and put off starting that business because—dang, that's stressful!

But when we live unconsciously, we're left at the end of our lives asking, "For what?"

When I die, I want to feel that my time was well-spent. One creepy-sounding habit I have, when faced with a decision, is to ask myself, "When I'm on my deathbed, what will I want to remember?" For example, if I'm facing the decision of whether to accept a speaking engagement that makes me want to throw up with fear, I ask myself what I'll want to remember when I'm on my way out of this earthly plane—that I didn't throw up, or that I stood in front of 100 people and gave a talk that motivated them to start a writing business?

Will I want to remember that I carefully stewarded my time and energy to try to maintain a constant, never-ending sense of calm? That I let fear and lack of energy keep me from going after my D-I-A Desires and making an impact? Or that I traveled the world with my family, ran a business I loved, started a non-profit that helped animals, did a ton of entertaining, and generally had an amazing time?

The answer is pretty clear: I'd rather look back on a life filled with fun, family, learning, and action. I *won't* want to have my mind, in my last moments, filled with memories of boredom, lethargy, years of time-wasting activities, dreaded obligations, and living someone else's values and dreams, all the while wishing I'd accomplished more.

In an interview on Mindful.org, Bronnie Ware, a palliative care nurse and author of *The Top Five Regrets of the Dying*, noticed that when she talked with patients who were on their deathbeds, "That first regret—'I wish I'd had the courage to live a life true to myself'—kept coming up."

Do not let this happen to you.

Asking what we will want to remember on our deathbed is a way of bringing what are usually unconscious, automatic decisions into our consciousness, where we can examine them and then make the most fulfilling choices.

Chapter 10

Take the Drug

What if there were a free drug with zero side effects that would not only make you feel great, improve your health, boost your libido, focus your thinking, increase your self-esteem, and slim you down—but also give you more time?

Well, there is one. It's called *exercise*.

I can hear you now: "Wait, I already know exercise is good for my health and my mood, but did you just say it can give me more time? You must be on something, and it's not exercise." But yes, exercise can actually make you so energetic and productive that you get much more done in much less time. I've experienced this myself, and in my stint as a wellness coach I saw it happen for my clients, as well.

Counterintuitively, exercise makes you *less* tired, not more, which can also help you get more done. According to the book *Spark: The Revolutionary New Science of Exercise and the Brain*: "In 2004, researchers at Leeds Metropolitan University in England found that workers who used their company's gym were more productive and felt better able to handle their workloads. Overall, they felt better about their work and less stressed when they exercised. And they felt less fatigued in the afternoon, despite expending energy at lunchtime."

Spend half an hour working out and you gain back at least a couple hours in increased productivity, which is why movement should be part of your D-I-A Plan, even when you're not working on the D-I-A Desire *Cross a Finish Line*.

But Exercise Sucks!

Do you know why exercise sucks? It's because instead of making it work for you, *you* work for *it*. You slog on the treadmill, hating every second of it, because you want to burn off those nasty calories. Or you lift five-pound weights for 50 reps, just so you can say you did it and get on with your day already.

But if you make it work for you, exercise is a glorious thing. Here's an example: Today an editor pissed me off. She asked to schedule a call yesterday at 1 pm to discuss a possible assignment. I raced home from the bookstore, where I was working on another project, and dutifully called at one on the dot. No answer. I called again 15 minutes later, and tried the editor's cell, as well. No response. I waited another half hour before moving on to other work.

Today, after I prompted her via e-mail, the editor apologized that yesterday was a "Typical Monday," and am I available today at one instead?

Seething, I ditched my planned bodyweight workout in favor of yoga, concentrating on heart-opening postures, plus twists to work out the anger, and a few simple inversions to help boost my mood. *Voila*—I went from angry to okay, and I got in a good workout at the same time.

Another example: The other day I had planned to work on this book, but was feeling simultaneously anxious and lethargic. I already had a yoga session planned, but decided to walk downtown to the studio instead of driving in order to get a hit of sun and some heart rate-boosting cardio. By the time I left the studio, I felt perfectly at ease and energetic again, and managed to write another two chapters.

You don't have to stick to a regimented workout schedule just because it seems like the normal thing to do. You're more likely to actually exercise if you go with what inspires you and what your body tells you that *you* need, than if you tell yourself, "Ugh, I *have* to get in a cardio workout today because it's Tuesday." Once you start enjoying exercise for what it can do for you, you'll probably do plenty of it during your week. You may even find yourself toning up and slimming down, even though your main purpose for exercising is to increase your energy and lift your mood.

The D-I-A Exercise Non-Plan

So how does this help in terms of doing it all? Basically, you do whatever kind of movement will get you in the right state to go after your current D-I-A Desire. For example:

- You have a crowd of people coming over as part the D-I-A Desire *Entertain*, but you're upset at something your spouse said and wishing you didn't have to put on a happy face for a bunch of guests in an hour. So you go for a brisk walk around the block, listening to soothing music or just looking at the trees, and by the time you get back, you've worked out that raw, angry feeling.
- Your current D-I-A Desire is *Learn Mad Skills*, but your eyelids start drifting shut every time you try to focus on your class homework. You blast techno music, take a few deep breaths, and pump out ten minutes of pushups, squats, and jumping jacks. Energy restored!
- Now your D-I-A Desire is *Volunteer*, so you offer to help out at a local animal shelter. Some of the situations you see make you so sad that you're not sure you want to go back. You head to a yoga class at the local studio or do a YouTube routine at home, and finish it off with ten minutes of meditation. Seeing neglected, homeless, and abused pets in a shelter is still upsetting, but now you feel you can handle it with grace and love.
- For the D-I-A Desire *Start a Side Hustle*, you're so anxious over the idea of failing at your new business that you can't focus, and you find yourself surfing social media instead of writing your business plan. So you pump some heavy weights and run around the block to work out the negative energy, and when you get back, you're feeling much more centered and focused, and ready to take a crack at that business plan.

Do what you naturally gravitate toward based on your mood, and not only will exercise not suck anymore, it will become a valuable part of your D-I-A life.

Chapter 11

Build Your Energy

You may be working a day job. You might also have a partner, kids, and pets. Add a D-I-A Plan to the mix and you have a recipe for one extra-crispy woman.

That's why it's key to take care of yourself while you're working on your D-I-A Plan.

If taking the time to give yourself attention seems a wee bit selfish when you have so many other beings who need you, whether it's your boss or your kids or your cat, listen up: If you don't take great care of yourself, you won't have as much energy for your D-I-A Plan. As you remember, doing it all will benefit not just you, but also those around you—but only if you keep yourself as rested, happy, and healthy as possible throughout the Plan.

Another popular objection: "If I don't have time for some of these D-I-A Desires, I certainly don't have time to get a massage or go for a leisurely jog in the park." But believe it or not, when you make the time to do some of the self-care practices below, you'll find that *you actually get more done during the day*. This is the same phenomenon we discussed in Chapter 10, *Take the Drug*.

You may feel like you're wasting that half hour meditating, taking a bath, or making a big salad—but you'll go back to your work, your family, and your D-I-A Plan with such renewed energy that it takes you only a fraction of the usual time to complete your tasks. I've experienced this myself, and so have many of my clients.

Here are some self-care practices that will keep your body and mind strong and energetic, so you can create a rich life full of memories and purpose.

Stop Eating Junk

You're so busy with your D-I-A Plan that you only have time to down a handful of cheese curls and a swig of Diet Coke for lunch. It wouldn't be so bad if you hadn't skipped breakfast. And as for dinner—honey, can you pick up some Wendy's on your way home from work...again?

We've all been there. It's understandable that you have little time to prepare healthy meals when you're focused on your D-I-A Desires. But fueling your body well is crucial if you want to have the energy to keep all those balls in the air.

We tend to resort to pat excuses why we can't eat well, like "I have no time," "It's expensive," or "I can't resist junk food." Ask yourself exactly what your obstacle to eating well is, and brainstorm creative ways around it.

For example, if your excuse is "I don't have time to shop for healthy food," you could:

- Explore once-a-month shopping, and try keeping your pantry stocked with healthy eats.
- Ask your significant other to do the shopping.
- Have your groceries delivered using a service like Peapod.
- Order your groceries online and then pick them up. Many grocery stores offer this service at a low price.
- Stock your kitchen with long-lasting healthy foods like root vegetables, citrus fruits, eggs, pasta, sauces, canned goods, and frozen veggies so you don't have to shop as often.

Or if "I hate cooking" is the excuse that makes you want to add the Chinese delivery joint to your speed dial, you could:

- Stock up on healthy frozen dinners.
- Trade off cooking with your partner.
- Get your kids to take turns preparing simple meals.

- Visit a meal assembly kitchen, where you prepare a week's worth of meals to heat up at home.
- Brainstorm a list of super-simple but healthy foods you can prepare in no time, like scrambled eggs, oatmeal, and pre-cut fruits and vegetables with hummus.
- Learn how to create healthy meals in a slow cooker or electric pressure cooker. The appliance does all the work for you!
- Make your meals for the week on Sunday and freeze them, so you get all the dreaded cooking out of the way at once.
- Organize a dinner club with your friends. Each person makes enough batches of one meal for all the members of the group, then you all exchange meals. You only have to make one dish, but you get a week's worth of dinners.

No matter what your excuses are when it comes to fueling your body so you can work better, there are always solutions if you think creatively.

Also, keep in mind that the diet that's best for your spouse or your BFF may not be the one that's best for you. We're all different. My husband takes three fish oil capsules per day, but when I pop even one, my hands and feet hurt like crazy for the next 24 hours. Some people swear by a Paleo diet, others by veganism. Know yourself...and if you don't, experiment.

Say *Om*

It takes only five minutes. Sit quietly and count your breaths. When a thought arises, watch it, but don't engage.

Short meditation breaks can help you get centered on a crazy-busy day, create energy, and make room for D-I-A inspiration to flow in.

I know it's not easy to take the time to meditate when you have so much going on. But as the Zen proverb goes, "You should sit in meditation for twenty minutes every day, unless you're too busy. Then you should sit for an hour."

If you could use help concentrating, I recommend the free, guided meditation podcasts from TheMeditationPodcast.com, which use soothing background sounds, alpha wave audio technology, and guided imagery to help you focus on the meditation.

Get Away From It All

You've had it. You've been working, taking care of your family, and working on your D-I-A Plan, and you're burned out.

This is the time to take a break—maybe a big one. You may hope to plow through the exhaustion, but doing this only sets you up for a crash, or even illness. Giving yourself time to recover will make you even more productive when you get back to your D-I-A Plan. Have you ever felt supremely productive when trying to bash through exhaustion using brute force? Neither have I.

For example, as I mentioned earlier, I wrote part of this book from a hotel because I was *truly* ready to poke my eyes out with a Sharpie. I stayed two nights, and the first day I ordered room service, never left the room, and wrote all day. The second day, I relaxed in the hotel spa, had breakfast, and then wrote some more. After a period of frustration, writer's block, and holy-moly-leave-me-alone-or-my-brain-will-explode-all-over-you, this quick trip helped me regain my inspiration and energy, and boosted my mood back up to pre-Sharpie-stabbing levels.

Breaks can be anywhere from a few minutes to a weekend or more, and they don't have to cost anything. Try these when you've hit a wall:

- Take a stretch break.
- Go for a walk on a hiking trail.
- Take the weekend off and do zero work.
- Go on a cheap vacation by visiting a friend who lives within driving distance.
- Relax on the sofa with a bestseller.
- Go by yourself to a café, and enjoy a ridiculously frothy coffee drink.
- Call a friend for an hour-long BS session.
- Watch your favorite movie.
- Take a nap.

Do not feel guilty for needing a break. Even if we want to do it all, we humans aren't made for non-stop work. If stress, exhaustion, or overwhelm are tempting you to round-file your Plan for good, rest until you're ready again and then get back to it.

Believe You Can

If you don't really believe you can make your D-I-A Desires a reality, your energy will plummet and helpfully make that negative belief come true for you. According to the book *Maximum Brainpower: Challenging the Brain for Health and Wisdom* by Shlomo Breznitz and Collins Hemingway, that's because: "The brain does not want the body to expend its resources unless we have a reasonable chance of success. Our physical strength is not accessible to us if the brain does not believe in the outcome, because the worst possible thing for humans to do is to expend all of our resources and fail. If we do not believe we can make it, we will not get the resources we need to make it. The moment we believe, the gates are opened, and a flood of energy is unleashed. Both hope and despair are self-fulfilling prophecies."

So how do you believe you can do it all...when you really don't? One way is to develop a mindset that values *completion,* not *perfection.* In other words, believing you can do something does not mean believing you can do it *perfectly,* but believing you can *finish the project* or reach the goal, no matter how many times you muck it up along the way.

Perfection leads to endless lists and a slew of incomplete projects, because they're never done until they're perfect, and we all know there's no such thing as perfect. Your body knows perfection is impossible, so your energy drops, and that seals the fate of your D-I-A Plan. What matters most is your ability to start *and complete* a D-I-A Goal. Finishing is winning. The results may not be perfect—maybe you hosted a party and ran out of those delicious prosciutto-brie toasts, or screwed up on the first day of your new volunteer gig—but if you got through it alive, you're golden. Believe this and your body will cooperate by providing the resources you need.

Do Something, Anything!

Your first instinct when it comes to boosting your energy may be to conserve it though a marathon couch-sitting session. However, the American Psychological Association says the *least* effective ways to deal with stress are gambling, shopping, smoking, drinking, eating, playing video games, surfing the internet, and watching TV and movies for more than two hours.

What does work? According to the APA, it's activities like exercise, meditation, being with friends, praying or attending a religious service, getting a massage, and listening to music. Do some of these sound like D-I-A Goals to you?

When your energy is at its nadir, resist the natural impulse to zone out with something mindless. Doing something interesting, active, or inspiring will give you the energetic boost to go after your D-I-A Desires with renewed vigor.

Chapter 12

Recalibrate

Here's how many of us manage our stress: Run run run run run. Crash. Consume a gallon of rocky road ice cream and wash it down with coffee. Feel better. Run run run run run. Crash.

Your D-I-A Plan will require steady energy and positive habits—after all, the Plan is about making you *happy*—so this cycle is the opposite of what you want.

We already talked about how acute stress isn't all bad, but you don't want it to develop into that constant, low-level hum of anxiety that can make you sick. Here's a way to keep the positive energy flowing steadily, and to keep the stress from becoming overwhelming: Instead of waiting until the inevitable crash before finally taking care of yourself, make small, frequent recalibrations so you never get to that crash in the first place.

For example:

- Meditate for 20 minutes every evening.
- Take a hot bath as soon as you feel that telltale tension in your shoulders.
- Down an immune-booster vitamin powder drink and go to bed early the day you sense the first signs of a cold.
- Get a massage, even if you don't need one to destress…yet.
- Read a chapter of an inspirational book every morning.
- Check the calendar. In talking with many women, I discovered I'm not the only one who wonders why she feels anxious and irritable, looks at the calendar, and realizes, "Oh yeah, it's almost

that time of the month." Seriously, you'd think we'd learn after however many years. Just knowing why you're feeling peevish can go a long way toward ameliorating it.
- Write in your journal to work out problems *before* you get to the point where you want to poke your eyes out with a Sharpie.

If you recalibrate often, your energy and stress levels will have small, manageable ups and downs—instead of giant spikes where you run your butt off for a week and then need to sleep for three days straight.

Chapter 13

Change the Way You Talk

A downfall many women have is that we really want to go all-out toward our D-I-A Desires, but we feel demotivated, uninspired, stuck, sad, angry, overwhelmed, or just plain *blah*. We get upset that our goals aren't happening as quickly as we'd like, or we're anxious because doing it all can be uncomfortable at times—and who likes to be uncomfortable?

One solution is to shake up your dialog. The words you choose when you talk to yourself, and to others, have a huge impact on how you feel and act. If you think or talk about your D-I-A Plan using negative, weak, or sad-sounding words, the Plan will feel like a downer as well, instead of your ticket out of boredom, lethargy, and passivity.

Here are several language-based strategies that can help you go from *ugh* to *yay!*

Think *And* Instead of *Or*

We often feel like we're being torn in two: Do I make good money *or* work a job I love? Do I work a job I love *or* stay at home with the kids? I have time to train for a 5k *or* volunteer, but not both. I have the money to create a home I love *or* travel.

Here's a mind shift I read about in the newsletter of Chip and Dan Heath, authors of *Made to Stick: Why Some Ideas Survive and Others Die*: "Always try to think AND not OR. Can you avoid choosing among your options and try several at once? For instance, if you're deciding whether to invest time in Spanish lessons or ballroom dancing classes, do both for a while until one of them wins. Or, rather than hire one employee out of three candidates, could you give all three a 2-week consulting project so that you can compare their work on a real-world assignment?"

When you change *or* to *and*, you get options like this:

- I plan to find a job that I love *and* that pays well.
- I'll look for a job that will let me telecommute, *and* I can stay at home with the kids.
- What if I volunteered to do setup for a charity race? Then I could volunteer *and* train!
- I'm looking for a hobby that combines my love of foreign languages *and* painting. How about offering to teach a painting class at the Chinese Community Center?
- I want to travel *and* save the money to create the kitchen of my dreams. Let me look at our budget to see what expenses we can cut, and also explore travel hacks for scoring cheap airfare.

You get the idea: Using the word *and* instead of *or* opens up possibilities in your life that you may never have considered before, and that can help make your D-I-A Plan a reality.

Think *And* Instead of *But*

What's the difference? The word *but* shuts down any hope for a solution, and gives you an easy out when it comes to your D-I-A Goals. Replace *but* with *and*, and suddenly you're open to brainstorming new options. For example:

1. "I want to become well-read, *but* I don't have money for books." Do you hear the *It is what it is* here?
2. "I want to become well-read, *and* I don't have money for books." Now your mind automatically goes on to ask, "So what can I do? Maybe I can go to the library, borrow books from a friend, download free public-domain classic novels, or join a book swap!"

I'd say you should try this tactic, but then I'd have to contradict myself with…

Do or Do Not. There is No *Try*.

When you tell yourself or others that you'll try to do something, here's what you're really saying: "I have no confidence I can accomplish this goal, or I don't want to do it but don't know how to say no." Consider these two statements to your running group leader:

1. "I'll try to make it to the running group today to train for my 5k."
2. "I'll see you at the running group today to train for my 5k."

See the difference? In the first sentence, you're conveniently leaving yourself an out: "Well, I said I'd *try*, but something else came up. Sorry!" Yoda had it right: Say you're going to do something, and then do it.

Instead of Saying *I Have to* or *I Should*, Say *I'm Going to* or *I Get To*

You're talking with your best gal pal about your current D-I-A Desire and are about to say, "This morning I have to meditate," or "I really should find somewhere to volunteer today." Instead say, "This morning I get to meditate!" Or, "I'm going to find somewhere to volunteer today!" Do you feel the difference?

Though it will take repeated efforts, you can do the same in your own head. When you catch yourself thinking, "Ugh, I have to work on the website for my side gig today," grab yourself by the gray matter, shake it around a little, and tell yourself instead, "Today I get to work on the website for my new side gig! Yippee!"

This isn't really a mind trick, because it's totally true. You're alive! You're in the envied position of being able to meditate, start a new business, and volunteer. You *get* to do all these things. You are so lucky!

Rename Your Tasks

This idea comes from the book *Level Up Your Life: How to Unlock Adventure and Happiness by Becoming the Hero of Your Own Story* by Steve Kamb: Instead of calling the to-dos on your list *tasks*, call them something that makes them sound way more exciting, like *mini-quests* or *adventures*. Remember, everything on your to-do list should be there to further your D-I-A Desires, make you happy, and improve your life!

Minimize Your Emotional Language

And this idea I borrowed from Tony Robbins: Whenever you feel a strong negative emotion bubbling to the surface of your consciousness, tone down the words you use to describe it. In fact, tone them *way* down.

For example, instead of saying you're *extremely overwhelmed* at everything you want to do for your D-I-A Plan, tell yourself, "I'm feeling just a tad nervous." If you're *furious* that your Plan isn't going as well as you'd hoped, say, "I'm slightly annoyed that the competition I trained for was cancelled." *Devastated* that your partner isn't showing you the support you were hoping for? Say, "I'm a little disappointed my partner isn't as excited about my D-I-A Plan as I am."

Along the same lines, a trick I learned long ago is to replace the words *nervous*, *anxious*, or *stressed* (and anything related to them) with *excited*. So now you're *excited* about that speaking engagement, not *petrified*. And you're not *stressed* about that upcoming certification exam...you're *excited*!

Toning down your emotional words defuses the emotions attached with them, as well. And sometimes it even makes you laugh, defusing the emotions even more: Imagine the chuckle you'll get out of the understatement *I'm a tad annoyed* when you're really in Sharpie-poking mode.

Words have power, and the way you talk to yourself and others can boost your motivation—or destroy it. Try these tricky strategies for changing up your language, and you'll feel empowered, inspired, and excited to go after your D-I-A Desires.

Chapter 14

Go Back for the Future

Marty McFly was on to something: Being stuck in the past can motivate you to go after the big, fat D-I-A life you've been dreaming of.

This is from a study referenced in *The 100 Simple Secrets of Successful People* by David Niven, Ph.D.: "Comparing people who tend to give up easily with people who tend to carry on, even through difficult challenges, researchers find that persistent people spend twice as much time thinking, not about what has to be done, but about what they have already accomplished, the fact that the task is doable, and that they are capable of it."

I was being facetious about the *stuck in the past* thing, but the truth is, looking back on your accomplishments and moments of pride will actually benefit you. Here's one way to do that:

Make a *Did List*

Many of my clients tell me that what they love most about my mentoring form is answering the question, "What did you accomplish in the last week?"

Why? Because many days we feel like did nothing but spin our wheels, but when we write a list of what we got done, it's always more than we think. Nothing boosts your confidence like feeling accomplished and productive!

When I mentioned this to a client, she came up with the idea of a daily *What I Got Done List*, which I like to call a *Did List*. Instead of

[si]mply crossing things off your to-do list as you complete them, you can enter them into your *Did List*.

I like to use this list when I feel like I'm putting out fires all day and getting zero done. Like today: Even though I got up at 4:30 am, I felt like I was getting nothing done all day long...but here's what my *Did List* looked like at the end of the day:

- Edited this book for two hours before sun-up.
- Completed Week 1, Day 1 of the Couch to 5k podcast. (It was 28° F this morning…great day to start!)
- Cleaned up the house.
- Took my son to school.
- Looked up resources for learning Chinese for a trip we're planning.
- Wrote this chapter.
- Answered important e-mails.
- Ordered and picked up groceries.
- Had coffee with a friend.
- Managed a contest for my readers.
- Wrote and set up a motivational email for my Write for Magazines e-course students.
- Helped my son make Valentine's Day cards for his classmates.
- Read a few chapters of a new book.
- Contacted our county's housing division and got suggestions for three homeless shelters that may be interested in having my family host a board game day.
- Made dinner.
- Took our exchange student to the ATM.

I felt a lot better after writing that list, when before I was doubting my ability to accomplish even the smallest tasks.

Of course, I included a *Did List* Worksheet in this book! This is one you can use every single day if you want to, or only when you need a boost. Seeing everything you've accomplished, as research confirms, will help you keep on rocking with your D-I-A Plan.

Chapter 15

Change Your Mind

If you're afraid to attempt everything you really want to do, remember: Nothing is permanent.

If there are parts of your D-I-A Plan that you've committed to, and you come to realize you don't like them, you can stop doing them. That's right—though I ask you to give each of your Desires or Goals a fair try, you can always make adjustments!

I'm a Serial Quitter, and Proud of It

When I was in graduate school, I applied for a government internship in Bulgaria. I didn't get it. Those Bulgarians didn't know what they were missing! But as part of the application, I had to list every job I'd ever had up to that point.

Of course, this being a government position, the security screening was intense. The people in charge of the program called my friends, family members, and neighbors to make sure I wasn't some sort of terrorist. When they called my mom, they asked, "Has Linda really had 26 jobs?" To which my mom replied, "Yep." I had worked in retail, held office jobs, waitressed, held a position as a telemarketer for less than a day, and freelanced as an indexer, translator, and tutor, before finally discovering my calling as a writer. If I hadn't had *and* quit all those jobs, who knows what I'd be stuck doing right now?

Another example: In 2007, besides writing full-time for magazines, authoring books, teaching classes, mentoring writers, and studying martial arts, I decided I also wanted to start an animal welfare organization called creativePAW. I had a website built, grew a list of over 400 volunteers, and marketed our *pro bono* services to shelters all over the US. I fielded requests for help by the dozen, and received many emails from happy shelter managers about how much my volunteers had helped them.

After a couple years, running the organization started to feel like a grind. I had a baby now, and my freelance writing was picking up even more. As much as I cared about animal welfare, creativePAW was no longer a priority. I wrote to my 400 volunteers, asking if anyone would like to take over the organization, interviewed a few good prospects, and handed over the reins to someone I thought would do a good job. She ran it for a few more years, helping many more shelters in the process. Although creativePAW no longer exists, I discovered that one of the groups creativePAW helped created a copycat organization. CreativePAW, and all the good it did, is still part of my life's resume and my legacy.

One final example: In 2011, I decided to switch gears and become a personal trainer and wellness coach. I took a 13-week wellness coaching certification course, hired my own life coach and personal trainer to give me pointers, studied for and earned my personal training certification, rented and stocked a training studio, gave away free personal training and wellness coaching sessions, landed some clients, trained them for six months…and then thought, "Meh." Once I decided this career path wasn't for me, I sublet the studio, sold the equipment, and got back to my writing. Though now I could tell health magazine editors I was a certified personal trainer, because the certification lasted two years!

But Don't Really Call It Quitting

I was being tongue-in-cheek when I said I'm a serial quitter. I prefer to call it *experimenting*, not *quitting*. You can either do new things and discover whether you want them as a permanent part of your life, or never do anything at all, so at least people won't be able to call you a quitter.

Remember Chapter 8, *Inconsistency Is A-OK*? That applies not only to the D-I-A strategies in this book, but to your D-I-A Goals, as well.

Consider *your* D-I-A Plan an experiment. It's your Plan, so you can tweak it as needed: Add things, drop things, or even back off altogether, if you gave a Goal a good run and realize you simply don't want it in your life. That's right: You can stop. At any time. Just like that.

It's not all or nothing, and you can always change your mind. Remember that whatever you try will always be part of your history...a history you'll look back on with pride.

Chapter 16

Practice Extreme Gratitude

You've heard the advice to start a gratitude journal more times than you can count. If you're not doing it by now, there's probably a good reason. Maybe you know deep inside it wouldn't help you right now, you're having trouble with the concept of gratitude ("Gratitude for what? For having a cold, a demanding boss, and a whiny kid?"), or you're just not that into it.

Or it may be that whatever you try to do, it seems like everyone is trying to stop you, and the universe is throwing obstacles in your way. You go to borrow a book from the library for your *Become Well-Read* Desire, and there's a three-month waiting list. You order Japanese language-learning materials, and the package gets lost in the mail. You try to fulfill your D-I-A Desire *Entertain* and ten people show up to your ugly sweater party without RSVPing, so you have to scramble feverishly for more appetizers and favors. What's there to be grateful about?

If your D-I-A motivation is being derailed by feelings that the world is against you, I know a different kind of gratitude practice that can help more than ye olde gratitude journal.

Let's use the Desire *Become Well-Read* as an example. Say you're reading a biography of some historical figure on an e-reader like a Kindle, Nook, or iPad. Now, stop and think about that book. To get the biography into your hands, a writer, editor, proofreader, book cover designer, e-book designer, publicity team, and more worked for weeks and weeks; employees at the utilities company sent electricity to all of these people's homes and businesses, and also to your home to charge that e-reader; other people designed, built, marketed, pack-

aged, transported, and sold the device you're reading th
at the plastics and metals manufacturing plants created
that make up your device; workers at the Mint printed the mon
used to buy this book; and if your e-reader is clad in a leather cover, an animal gave its life for that. Thousands of strangers worked countless hours in order for *you* to enjoy a book as part of your D-I-A Plan.

Feeling less like the world is against you now?

The exercise above is part of a form of Japanese therapy called *Naikan*. The basic structure of Naikan therapy involves asking yourself three questions:

1. What did I receive from others today?
2. What have I given to others today?
3. What troubles and difficulties did I cause others today?

The beauty of this exercise is that you can do it anywhere, you can focus on current activities or past events, and you can reflect on different people in your life. And, unlike the traditional generic gratitude journal, it can help you in your D-I-A quest by showing you in undeniable detail how much support you really have in your life, which offers a happiness boost, with a dose of motivation to boot. There are many more people (and animals, and things) helping you than hindering you in your goals.

A Naikan practice can help derail the inevitable stress of a D-I-A life, too. Though Naikan wasn't developed as a mental health exercise, Japanese therapists have found that Naikan therapy does help treat mental health issues like depression and anxiety. For example, 65% of participants in a 2004 study were less depressed after intensive Naikan therapy, and a 2005 study concluded that Naikan therapy is extremely effective for helping people with panic disorder and generalized anxiety disorder.

The first time I tried this Naikan exercise, I was shocked to discover that:

1. Despite my carping whenever the universe doesn't conform to my expectations, I'm being nurtured and served by thousands of people, animals, and things.

2. If I were to create a pie chart, the section for *Linda Receives* would dwarf the tiny slice that says *Linda Gives*.
3. I cause inconvenience to others in a multitude of ways, from holding up a line of caffeine-deprived people while digging for change at the café register, to ousting a cat from its sleeping place so I can sit.

When it comes to powering your D-I-A attitude, it makes sense to reflect on what you received from others and what you've given to others on any given day. But why bother with reflecting on how you've inconvenienced others—unless you want to give yourself a guilt complex? I once interviewed Gregg Krech, author of *Naikan: Gratitude, Grace, and the Japanese Art of Self-Reflection*, and he told me that even if we recognize and appreciate all that we receive every day, we still tend to have a sense of entitlement—a sense that we earned and deserve these things. Being aware of the mistakes we've made and the suffering we've caused in the world can increase our gratitude quotient.

That sense of gratitude leads to a bump in energy and motivation, according to an article on Gaia.com—perfect for your quest to do, experience, and see all the awesome and fun stuff you can cram into your life. I've included a Naikan worksheet in this book. Test out a daily practice and see if it helps you feel better, get motivated, and get more done that will let you craft a rich and rewarding life.

Chapter 17

Become More Intolerant

There's a spot on the rug. I hate my hair. The dog keeps jumping on the bed. I don't like the way the phone rings. Life coach Kristin Taliaferro says women zap their energy by putting up with the multitude of little things that bother them every day, which coaches call *tolerations*. For the woman who is going after a big, marvelous D-I-A life, tolerations are pure evil.

Tolerations do more than drain your energy. They also clutter your life to such an extent that you have no time or mental space for anything else, including your D-I-A Plan. "Getting rid of tolerations opens up space so good things can flow in," Kristin says.

Here's how to give the heave-ho to tolerations, so you can move along with your Plan:

Make a List, Check It Twice

Kristin suggests jotting down 100 things in your life that bug you to no end. Don't be surprised at how quickly you reach this mark. Years ago when Kristin instructed me to compile a lengthy list of my tolerations, I was skeptical. But to my surprise, I came up with 65 in under half an hour, and brought the count up to 100 the next day.

To think that there are so many little things that make my blood boil! Examples:

- "The fridge is noisy."
- "I still haven't heard back from the life insurance guy."

- "The hostas are dying."
- "I don't like my doctor."

I now keep a running list of tolerations on my laptop that I add to and delete from as needed.

There are several places in your life where tolerations hide out, so examine each of these areas as you write your list:

Your health: The most-often ignored area of tolerations is around self-care, Kristin says, which makes it the best place to start. Sick of voicemails from your PCP reminding you that you're overdue for your mammo? Suffering from untreated allergies? Taking care of your health problems will make you feel great, which will make it that much easier to blast through the rest of your tolerations.

Your home: Go through each room in your home seeking out tolerations. Do you hate that melted spatula, noisy microwave, leaky pitcher in the kitchen? In the bathroom, does the moldy grout drive you out of your mind, not to mention the shampoo bottle with the cap that's impossible to open without superhuman strength?

Your career: The cubicle mate who snaps her gum, the co-worker who steals your ideas, constant interruptions, long hours that cause you to miss your daughter's soccer games—these are all sapping you of energy every day.

Your equipment and appliances: Crashing laptops, temperamental clothes dryers, a cracked smartphone, and a dirty car are all examples of big tolerations.

Your environment: Think junk mail in your mailbox, spam that gets through your filters, noisy neighbors, and light that leaks through the bedroom blinds at night.

Your time: Then there are the time-sapping tolerations like traffic jams, train delays, friends who are always late, and long lines at the supermarket.

Your relationships: As much as we love them, friends and relatives often have habits that grate on our nerves, such as making backhanded compliments or calling during dinner, and Kristin is a strong proponent of handling these tolerations, no matter how uncomfortable it may be for you at first.

Your finances: Debt, confusing bills from the phone company, low-paying freelance gigs, and the always-irritating lack of money all belong in this category.

Blast Them Away

Now comes the hard-but-fun part: Crossing your tolerations off the list one by one. You can vow to tackle the tolerations in one room every week, get rid of ten tolerations per week, or slay the most irritating ones first. Kristin likes the idea of eliminating tolerations by category, like health-related tolerations one week, and appliance-related tolerations the next, and reveling in the satisfaction and clarity that comes from having one area in your life clear of energy-draining distractions.

Kristin suggests coming up with three ways to do away with each toleration. For example, you could sew up a torn comforter cover yourself, hire someone else to fix it, or buy a new one. You could fix your own messy nails, get a professional manicure, or learn to be happy with ragged cuticles.

You may need to spend money to delete a toleration from your life, but many tolerations are cash-free fixes. For example, nixing time-related tolerations is often a simple matter of adjusting your timing—like going to the supermarket on Tuesday instead of on the busy weekend, leaving for your destination ten minutes earlier, or telling your habitually tardy friend that the movie starts 15 minutes earlier than it really does.

Banishing your tolerations will help you feel more motivated, energetic, and emotionally free, and give you the time and mental space to go after your D-I-A Desires. As part of your bonus downloads I have a Tolerations Worksheet where you can list 100 of the little buggers. Then, in the D-I-A Worksheets for each Desire, I'll be asking you to pinpoint the ones you'll be taking care of during that portion of the Plan. I also included a Killed Tolerations Worksheet where you can list the annoyances you deleted, so you can go back every so often and take pride in what you've accomplished (as we discussed in Chapter 14, *Go Back for the Future*).

PART 3

How to Cram It All In

"All the things we've seen and it's only eight in the morning!" —Flynn Rider

You're motivated, inspired, raring to go, and pretty much on fire to go after your D-I-A Desires.

But there's one problem: It's so hard to do it all when you feel like you barely have time to do the usual amount of stuff in your life! You're like, "How am I supposed to learn to play the viola when I don't even have two minutes to floss my teeth at night?"

In Part 3, you'll find tips on how to maximize the time you have, make even more time, and stop wasting this most precious resource.

Chapter 18

Get Support (But Not from Where You Think!)

Even with all the time-saving (or should I say time-*making*) advice I'll offer later in this book, if you want to live a truly D-I-A life, you can only do so much yourself. Sadly, you have time for only a finite number of physical actions in a day.

No matter how savvy you are with your Day Planner and Google Calendar, if you really want to do it all, chances are you'll need some help. Here's how to get it.

Lay Off Your Family

You've probably read this advice in magazines and online: "Get your kids to mop the floors! Ask your spouse to take charge of planning for birthdays!" Sounds good, right? It's about time those ingrates pitched in with the grunt work so you can do more *other* stuff.

But your kids don't care as much about the state of the bathroom floor as you do, so even if they do mop the tiles, you probably won't like the results. And your spouse doesn't give a darn if their mom is sent a birthday gift, and may not be interested in acting as your accountability partner when you train for a martial arts tournament.

Really, why should they? If maintaining a squeaky-clean house, or sending out 100 birthday cards every year, or training for an athletic event are part of your D-I-A Plan, that's *your* life vision, not theirs. If you want something done the way *you* want it done, you can do it yourself…or you can hire someone.

Believe me, I've been there. I care about what the outside of our home looks like, and my husband does not. After years of hearing him say, "I know, I know, I need to mulch/mow/trim," and never seeing it actually happen, I finally gave up and hired a landscaper. For just $80 they come by twice a month to mow, edge, trim, weed, and blow away the fallen leaves.

I thought, "All those years, I could have eliminated the frustration of fruitless nagging, and the annoyance of having to look at a trashy-looking yard, for $80 per month? Like, less than some people spend at Starbucks?" Yes, indeed.

I had the same experience in 2015 after back surgery. I wasn't able to lift a gallon of milk, much less a vacuum, so I hired a cleaning service to come by once a week until I was better. I actually enjoy cleaning, but after seeing how much cleaner the house was when they left, and how it took them less than half the time than when my family and I did it—and how I didn't have to listen to them gripe and moan, and didn't have to provide detailed instructions on how to properly dust the baseboards—I decided to make weekly housecleaning a regular part of our budget.

Before you ask: No, this is *not* letting your family off the hook.

Everyone in a household needs to contribute to it to the extent that they can. A 5-year-old can pick up their toys, put dirty clothes in the laundry basket, and set the table, but probably not do heavy construction work. I am not advocating that you let your loved ones watch YouTube videos every non-work/non-school hour of the day, while you keep the entire household afloat solo. The basic standards of housekeeping are the responsibility of everyone who lives in the home. I'm also not suggesting that your family members are dolts who can't be taught to competently load the dishwasher.

But I *am* advocating that you figure out what you can reasonably expect the people in your life to care about, and that you decide how much it's worth to you to have certain things done right, done on time, and done with no nagging. Let's face it—many people don't care about sending birthday cards, or the fact that the driveway has mildew on it, or about balancing the checkbook or clothes shopping or picking out window coverings. If you do, and these things are part of your

D-I-A Plan, then it's time to figure out a way to get them done to your satisfaction.

For example, our son has been trained to help set the dinner table, clear away his own plates and utensils after meals, dust, clean toilets, and sort his dirty clothes into the correct laundry baskets. But he does not put away laundry or sweep. My husband is great at fixing things around the house, planning parties, and folding the laundry. But giving a crap about the state of the lawn? Forget it.

Admit it: There are things *you* refuse to do because you simply hate doing them. I will not empty the dishwasher—that's our exchange student's job—or put away the laundry (that's for hubby to do). Eric and I both dislike financial chores, hence we have a financial planner and accountant.

Build Your Home Team

If you want to get it all done, but don't care who actually does some parts of it, there's no end to the types of help available out there. For example, on the low-cost and no-cost end, you can:

- Trade off with a friend to each do the chores the other one despises.
- Form a babysitting co-op through a site like BabysittingCoop.com or BabysitterExchange.com. I have done this myself.
- Join a community running group for free 5k training.
- Get a free business mentor through SCORE. Close to 150,000 entrepreneurs have been mentored through this organization!
- Barter your skill. For example, if you're an accomplished baker, trade a custom birthday cake for accounting help, errand running, or lawn work. Craigslist has a special section just for barter offers.
- Ask a pro friend for advice on nutrition, interior design, gardening, finances, and so on. I have tons of skilled friends who are happy to offer me tips *gratis*, and you probably do, too.
- Pay a teenager with a car to run errands for a few bucks.

If you want to hire professional help, there are even more options, such as:

- Online grocery shopping. Some stores deliver, too.
- Housecleaners.
- Landscapers.
- Event planners.
- Personal trainers.
- Photographers to take your family photos.
- Laundry services.
- Financial consultants.
- Accountants.
- Personal shoppers to refurbish your wardrobe, purchase gifts, etc.
- Virtual assistants.
- Nutritionists.
- Personal/business coaches.
- Researchers (if, say, you own your own business).
- Gutter cleaners/power washers/handymen.
- Interior decorators.
- Tailors or dressmakers.

The support you want to look for, of course, depends on your D-I-A Desire. If right now you're training for an epic glow run, a personal trainer, running coach, or nutritionist can help you get in shape and kick that Goal's butt. If your current D-I-A Desire is *Create an Amazing Home*, interior decorators, painters, handymen, and housecleaners will get you to your Goals fast...minus the major hassle of trying to DIY.

You *Can* Afford It

We're a middle-class family with a fluctuating income, and I've hired 15 of the professionals and services on the above list. I take private yoga lessons, have a life coach, and shop for groceries online. I've hired an online dressmaking service to sew a cloak for my husband's Snape Halloween costume; have hired virtual assistants to format and schedule my blog posts; and use an accountant to do our business taxes.

If this reminds you of those wealthy households in *Downton Abbey* with a full staff of butlers and footmen, let me reassure you that a lot of this is less expensive than you might think, and sometimes it even pays for itself.

For example, online grocery shopping where I live costs $99 per year for unlimited orders. I check off the items I want, get a call when the order is complete, drive seven-tenths of a mile to the store, and read a book (as per my *Become Well-Read* Desire) while an employee loads the bags into my car and runs my debit card.

It's not cheap considering I could haul my sorry butt a mile to the store and shop for free, but I've actually saved more than the money I've spent. When the store is out of a product, the shopper will often substitute a similar item for free. If they don't have the size I ordered, they'll give me the larger size for the same price. When I ask for extra-ripe bananas to make banana bread, they toss them in *gratis*, because otherwise they'd be thrown out. The store also offers special discounts for their online shopping subscribers, like their Cyber Monday offer of 20% off orders up to $500. I stocked up on $500 worth of non-perishables and the subscription paid for itself right there.

Other examples: An accountant is not cheap, but can save you mucho on your tax bill to make up for it. A personal trainer might charge $30 per half hour, depending on where you live. Two sessions per week costs less than the restaurant trips many families make on a regular basis, and think of the savings in health-care costs down the road!

Hiring pros can save you time, too. A full workout with a personal trainer takes just 30 minutes from start to finish, because you don't need to trek to the gym, check in, put your stuff in a locker, wait for the treadmill/ab machine/whatever to open up, work out, and then drive back home. A housecleaner saves you hours every week, and you can do something else with the time you would have spent scrubbing the bathtubs and mopping the floors. A business coach can save you *years*, because instead of learning by trial-and-error, and reading books, and searching the internet for info, you get the exact right information and advice for your situation in one hour-long session, so you can start making money stat.

Hire Someone or Do It Yourself?

At this point you're probably asking yourself, "Well, if I can't expect unconditional help from my loved ones, and this all is part of my D-I-A Plan, why not do it all myself? Then I'll get it all done the way I want *and* save money!"

Hey, if you can do every single thing on your D-I-A Plan by yourself, without wanting to *constantly* stab yourself in the eye with a Sharpie, more power to you! Remember, the subtitle of this book alludes to *occasional* episodes of wanting to poke your eyes out.

But consider a few things:

1. As good as you think you are at something, someone who does it professionally is sure to be faster and better.
2. Do you think you get brownie points for doing everything yourself when you don't have to? Here's a news flash: You don't.
3. Why not spread the wealth? By *wealth*, I mean the feeling of pride and accomplishment one enjoys from a job well done. We feel a swell of satisfaction from being able to do everything personally, and it can be hard to let that go. One article I recently read reported that a lot of women won't *let* their spouses make dinner or take care of the kids, because these women feel like their partner is encroaching on their domain, which makes them feel less useful. But everyone in your household wants to feel competent and useful, and letting them doesn't make *you* any less so.
4. It helps to separate your to-do list from the ultimate goal. You know the saying, "The journey is the destination?" Here I reply, "Horse feathers." In the D-I-A Plan, if you want to travel more, the main goal is the travel itself, not the travel planning. If you hire a travel agent to do the planning, you can use the time and energy you saved actually *traveling*.

Ready to enlist *actual* help, instead of being constantly disappointed that your family and friends don't care about your D-I-A Desires as much as you do? In the D-I-A Plan Worksheets, for each Desire you'll find a section asking you to brainstorm who you can hire to help you with that Desire, where to find them, and ways to afford help if it's not currently in your budget.

Chapter 19

Before To-Do, Try To-Don't

This book is about how to fit in all the things you want to accomplish, see, do, create, and learn in your life. But what about all those tasks crowding your schedule that are getting in the way of your D-I-A Plan? We all have tasks and obligations we despise with the white-hot passion of a thousand suns, and they drain the time and energy we need for our D-I-A Desires.

Life coaches often suggest we add these items to a *To-Don't List*. This is pretty much the opposite of a to-do list, meaning you write down the tasks you refuse to take on any longer. *Decision* literally means to *cut off*, so when you make the decision to go after a D-I-A life, you'll need to cut off from your list the junk that's obscuring your goals.

Sure, we can create a To-Don't List or even find one online, but it can be so darned hard to actually *write* anything on it. I mean, these tasks need to get done, right? We *should* do them, yes? I spoke with life coach Kristin Taliaferro about how to ditch the guilt of adding items to your To-Don't List, so you'll have more time and mental energy for your D-I-A Plan.

Stand Up For Your Rights

You have the right to say no to the tasks you detest doing. Quoting Kristin: "Women say, 'Can I really *not* volunteer at my son's school anymore, when every other mom does it?' If you don't feel like you have the right, your communication will come out in an angry, defensive way." On the flip side, when you feel you're within your right to put items on your To-Don't List—which, again, you are—your communication will be more gracious, making the transition from to-do to to-don't easier on everyone.

Make It All About You

Say you have a friend who calls every night to dish...and dish...and dish about her day. You've decided this is going on your To-Don't List so you can spend that time working on your art, but you feel guilty about potentially hurting your buddy's feelings. "Let her know what you're working on," Kristin suggests. "When you do that, you look vulnerable to her, so she actually *wants* to help you and she's not offended." For example, instead of going with your first impulse of not picking up the phone, hoping she'll eventually get the hint, you could tell your friend you're taking a Chinese brush painting class and need that hour to do your homework.

Negotiate

You may be able to come up with a solution that makes everyone happy. For example, if you do enjoy catching up with your friend, just not every night, you might suggest having lunch together once a month instead. However, Kristin warns against shifting your To-Don'ts. If you don't enjoy hearing from this person, don't simply shift the obligation into another time slot. Instead, let her know you're working on your art and can't talk as often. And if you feel bad about *that*, take another look at Chapter 9, *Die Before You Die*: Do you really want to be on your deathbed, remembering that you put up with daily chat sessions with someone you didn't like all that much, instead of creating the art you love?

Don't Over-Explain

If you're telling a good friend you'll no longer be chatting every day, go ahead and explain why. But if you're putting, say, a volunteer obligation you don't enjoy on your To-Don't List, you don't need to come up with a lengthy explanation for dropping it. "I'm sorry, but that no longer works with my schedule" is an all-purpose explanation that gets you out quick and doesn't invite argument. The more details you offer, the more ammo people have to shoot down your decision.

Give a Gift

Keep in mind that when you put something on your To-Don't List, you may actually make others happier. One of Kristin's clients felt she had to be the one to put her kids to bed every night, even though she was exhausted from working all day. Kristin recommended that the client ask her husband to take over bedtime twice a week. The client was nervous that her kids or her husband would rebel, but they ended up loving the time together. "Sometimes putting something on your To-Don't List is a gift for others," Kristin says.

Also, the items on your To-Don't List are there to give you time and mental space to go after your D-I-A Plan, and therefore to become a more active, productive, and joyful human being. One surefire way to ditch the guilt of adding items to the To-Don't List is to remember that your friends and family would rather have a partner, mom, or friend who is joyful and energetic, rather than an automaton who gets all the drudge work done.

Make an Omelet

You have to break a few eggs to make an omelet, literally and figuratively. If you make big changes in your life, whether it's stepping down as book club organizer or refusing to be a short-order cook for your family, some people will be upset. Accept that and know that, with time, the people affected will get over it—and maybe even appreciate it.

Have Faith

If you feel guilty adding certain items to your To-Don't List, such as not-quite-right clients or chores you dislike, remember that doing so will create space for better situations to enter your life. You've probably experienced this phenomenon yourself, but not realized what it was.

For example, you outsource the cleaning, and a friend invites you to stay at her vacation home in Florida. Or you (politely) dump a pain-in-the-butt client, and then win ten sessions with a business coach. Serendipity!

"When my clients give up things that aren't working for them, something more positive always shows up," says Kristin. "It's as if you're creating a vacuum to draw in better opportunities." The To-Don't List is the perfect complement to your D-I-A Plan…and the more items on it, the better.

I have a To-Don't List Worksheet for you in the bonus downloads, which you can fill out before starting work on each D-I-A Desire.

Chapter 20

Quit Social Media

Speaking of To-Don't Lists: Social media is something I recommend you put right at the top of the list. I quit social media in October 2015. Deactivated my Facebook page. Deleted my Twitter account. Killed my LinkedIn profile.

My work had become overwhelming, and I got to wondering whether there were any activities in my work life I didn't need to be doing. Are some activities crowding out more important tasks that will have a stronger impact on my life, career, and D-I-A Plan?

An obvious one to look at was social media. It's like a monster you can never feed enough:

- "I should post on Facebook."
- "I need to check Twitter in case someone sent me a DM."
- "How can I get more followers?"
- "Hey, here's another free webinar on how to make a million with Facebook ads!"
- "I better find some posts to fill my Buffer with."
- "How can I make my blog post images more Pinterest-friendly?"
- "Oh my God, I haven't checked LinkedIn in *days*."
- "Is my follower-to-following ratio on Twitter okay?
- "I better respond to all those @replies!"

Social media takes only a few minutes per visit, but it wasn't about the *amount* of time I spent there—it was about the *number of times* every day I felt the need to stop what I was doing, check into one of the many social media platforms, respond to messages or share something, and then try to get back on track with my original activity. The result was an overwhelming feeling of distraction and scattered thinking. And I'm not the only one: Research from the University of California, Irvine, concluded it can take 23 minutes to return to your original task after an interruption. Hardly a recipe for a successful D-I-A Plan.

Then there was the matter of being at people's beck and call in several different formats, not to mention feeling the need to learn about and implement every new social media marketing strategy some internet guru came up with.

I like to do and accomplish a *lot*. Was social media another one of those things I wanted to do and accomplish, or was it stopping me from doing and accomplishing more important things?

My initial, knee-jerk reaction was that I *needed* social media as a part of running my businesses. So before taking the leap, I started reading blog posts and articles on the topic, and ran across a post on the *Forbes* blog about how the author discovered his tweets actually brought very little return in the form of clicks onto his articles.

I immediately checked my Twitter stats and noticed that while many of my tweets were shared, few were actually clicked on. How does that even happen? People are sharing without reading first? Then I checked our website stats and realized something even more shocking: Of the 15,000+ unique monthly visitors to the *Renegade Writer Blog*, just 200 of them come from Twitter. That's a measly 1.3% of our visitors.

So I was convinced Twitter was not useful for me, business-wise, and I never used it for social purposes. LinkedIn was the same story: Too much time spent for too little return. But what about Facebook?

Lately, my experience on Facebook had been me fending off friend requests from people with fake names and photos; scrolling endlessly through political rants, click-bait posts, and photos of abused animals every time I was stuck on a word while working on a newsletter; and experiencing anguish every time I received a friend request from a student or reader. A year or so before, I had trimmed my FB friends list to actual friends, but still felt bad saying no to requests from writing acquaintances and clients.

The people whose news and photos I really wanted to see, and who were interested in my news and photos, were already connected with me by phone, by email, or in *real life*. At the point when I was considering shutting down my account, I hadn't posted in three weeks, and I was *not* inundated with messages from Facebook friends asking, "Where have you been? We miss your cat photos, brags about your son's ballet performances, and musings on the writing life!"

Then, the kicker: I came to realize that every time I posted a photo or update, I was secretly hoping a certain person-who-shall-not-be-named would see it and be in awe over how great my life was going.

Remember how I said a D-I-A Plan is not about beating other people, making them jealous, or exacting revenge? Making spite-posts on Facebook directly opposes the *spirit* of D-I-A.

Once I made the decision to free myself from social media (remember how *decision* means *to cut off*), I killed off all my accounts within a five-minute period. Boom!

I recently started a closed Facebook Group for fans and beta readers of this book, which meant I needed to reactivate my Facebook account. I hated having to reopen my profile, see all the notifications that had piled up, and have my old posts viewable to the public—so I decided to create a brand new, blank profile under a slightly different name, transfer ownership of the group to that profile, and then deactivate my old profile again. That way I could run a Facebook Group, but not bother with the rest of the platform.

I feel much more peaceful with so many fewer things to think about: I no longer have to worry about tweet chats, direct messages, friend requests, @messages, filling my Buffer with posts, scrolling through my feed reader looking for posts to Buffer, social media marketing, *learning* about social media marketing, and much, much more. My productivity has skyrocketed as well.

It's a nice feeling to do, see, or experience something amazing as part of my D-I-A Plan and not immediately think, "I should post this on Facebook/Twitter/whatever." After all, what's the point of trying to do it all if you're experiencing that *all* through a keyboard, or through the lens of your smartphone camera? Why be more concerned with getting clicks, comments, and likes—living your experiences through other people's eyes—than with enjoying your D-I-A Plan for its own sake?

Worried that people will cry themselves to sleep if you're no longer posting your views on gun control on Facebook, or quoting Thoreau on Twitter? It's been several months since I quit social media, and out of 300 Facebook friends, 500+ LinkedIn connections, and 6,000 Twitter followers, a big *two* people have emailed to ask where I've been. Learn from my harsh experience: Other people aren't as interested in you as you think.

Imagine how much more you'll be able to accomplish in your D-I-A Plan if you aren't scrolling through Facebook posts, tweeting links and jokes, Instagramming your restaurant meals, pinning crafts on Pinterest that you want to do but never will, and wondering whether you really know that guy enough to connect on LinkedIn.

You may be using social media as a way to connect, but most of those connections are pretty lightweight. In any case, *liking* the new-baby photos of someone you barely know hardly counts as connecting. Are you able to find another way of connecting that will help you reach your D-I-A Goals—like hosting dinner parties, taking a friend out for coffee, going to a speed-dating event, attending an industry conference, traveling with your family, starting a Meetup group, or volunteering at the local library?

This book is all about doing more, accomplishing more, and experiencing more. Give social media a hard look: Is it adding to your ability to do it all, or taking away from it? I know quitting social media is a hard step, and whether or not to take it is a personal decision. But remember you can always go back if you miss it...which I wager you won't.

Chapter 21

Stop Checking Your Email

I need to check my email at least 20 times per hour, and if I don't respond to emails immediately, the senders cry into their pillows all night long. People need me! They want me!

That was the delusion I labored under for years, and email pretty much ran my life. I still got tons done, but looking back, I can imagine how much more productive I could have been if I had not been obsessively clicking on the *Check Email* button.

How often do you check your email? Tell the truth, now. And how much would you get done toward your D-I-A Desires if you weren't constantly distracted by the blinking envelope icon?

Constant email checking may seem like a harmless habit, but it is supremely distracting, and drains the time, focus, and energy that are so important for your D-I-A Plan. Research published in the *International Journal of Information Management* found that 70% of emails were attended to within six seconds of arriving, and that it took an average of 64 seconds after each interruption to get back on task.

Who on God's green Earth requires a reply to an email in six seconds? I don't know what kind of job these people had that made them feel the need to jump on their email so fast, but I can only surmise that it involved red telephones and big scary buttons.

Why Is Email so Enticing?

In researching the phenomenon of email addiction—because that's what it really is—I discovered it works on the principle of the *variable schedule of rewards*. In the 1950s, psychologist B.F. Skinner conducted a study where mice would press a lever and receive a small treat, a big treat, or nothing at all. The mice that got a treat at random times, as opposed to those that scored a treat every time they pressed the lever, became compulsive about hitting that treat button.

From an article in TechCrunch: "Variable rewards come in three types and involve the persistent pursuit of: rewards of the tribe, rewards of the hunt, and rewards of the self. [...] Email, for example, is addictive because it provides all three reward types at random intervals. First, we have a social obligation to answer our emails (the tribe). We are also conditioned to know that an email may tell us information about a potential business opportunity (the hunt). And finally, our email seems to call for us to complete the task of removing the unopened item notification in a sort of challenge to gain control over it (the self)."

Most emails are pretty disappointing, in my experience, but every once in a while we receive one that contains goodies like praise, a new job, or a funny joke or internet meme, and that reinforces the constant need to check.

But I Need to Be Connected Non-Stop for My Job!

Multiple studies have shown that we don't need to check and answer work email as much as we think we do. Constant checking distracts us from the work our employers are paying us for, which is probably not responding to a barrage of electronic communication within six seconds, for eight hours straight.

I understand there are times when you really do need to check a lot. For example, right now my husband is going back and forth on email, setting up meetings for an overseas trade show. That's his whole task for the day, and he's been on email pretty much non-stop. And when I hold a sale, I need to be available to answer questions from potential customers. But in most cases, people check in way more than they need to.

In a study Cal Newport writes about in his excellent book *Deep Work: Rules for Focused Success in a Distracted World*, Harvard Business School professor Leslie Perlow convinced execs at the highly-connected Boston Consulting Group to require every team member to eschew email and instant messaging one day every workweek. Naturally, the team freaked out. They would lose clients! Their jobs were in jeopardy!

The big surprise was that the consultants ended up enjoying their jobs more, learning more, and delivering better products to clients, because they now had the time to really focus on their work instead of having to react to communications like Pavlov's dogs slobbering when they heard a bell.

In a 2012 study, researchers at the University of California, Irvine, and the US Army cut off email usage for 13 information workers for five days. Here's the conclusion: "Our results show that without email, people multitasked less and had a longer task focus, as measured by a lower frequency of shifting between windows, and a longer duration of time spent working in each computer window. Further, we directly measured stress using wearable heart rate monitors and found that stress, as measured by heart rate variability, was lower without email. Interview data were consistent with our quantitative measures, as participants reported being able to focus more on their tasks."

More focus *and* less stress? Sounds like a good thing for women who want to do it all!

If your employer truly expects you to be constantly connected, you may need to convince them to experiment with offering employees unconnected time during the workweek, so the employees can focus on bringing actual, quantifiable value to the company. But I'd wager that in many cases, the constant email checking is an imaginary requirement you put on yourself.

No One Needs You That Much

I recently conducted a study of my inbox and discovered something interesting: The vast majority of my emails were of the type that made me think, "Oh, crap." Most emails were from people who wanted something from me: People asking for free writing advice, trying to sell me things I don't need, asking to place ads for their online casino on our blog, pitching guest posts on topics that are irrelevant to the blog, requesting that I review their random product or novel, pitching their clients as magazine article sources, and frothing at the mouth over typos in my blog posts or Monday Motivation emails.

I used to believe that answering emails asking for free advice was part of my job. If someone ever bought one of our books, took one of our classes, or hired me as a mentor, I felt I was obligated to respond to their emails quickly and give them whatever they asked for. But over the years, I've become more of a curmudgeon in that respect. My new and improved attitude is that if someone buys a $5 book from me, in return they receive a $5 book. If they take a class, I give them my full attention until the class is over. That's what they paid for. Value served, transaction closed. I don't need to be on the hook forever because someone dropped $5 on a book three years ago.

I also felt the need to respond immediately to emails from my subscribers, but again: When people join the list, they get two free e-books and a free motivational email every Monday, not to mention occasional gifts just for being loyal subscribers. In exchange, I ask my subscribers to read an occasional email marketing one of our books or classes. I'd consider that a fair request.

Finally, I discovered that spending time answering individual emails kept me from creating new work—like books and classes—that could help hundreds or thousands of people. I was checking my email non-stop *for* work, only to be distracted *from* my work.

Once I came to this realization, I decided to become a hardcore email slacker. I hired a virtual assistant to remove all 900 instances of Diana's and my email addresses from our Renegade Writer blog posts. I deleted the email address from the Contact page, and have in its place a note about how we can't respond to emails because we're busy writing, but here are some great resources that might answer your questions. I check email a couple times per day, and unless something is urgent, I try to leave it for my admin day on Friday.

The result? So far, no complaints. I guess I'm not as important to all these people as I thought I was, because no one is crying into their pillow at night when they don't hear back from me. As Cal Newport writes in *Deep Work*, "Those with a minor online presence, such as authors, overestimate how much people really care about replies to their messages." Guilty as charged.

Also, sales of our books and courses have remained steady, and our subscriber base is growing at a faster clip. So the excuse that I needed to respond quickly and thoroughly to every email in order to keep our business afloat? Busted!

I'm Convinced. Now What?

So I've convinced you that constant email checking and answering is getting in the way of your D-I-A life. Now, I want to share the number one way to delete this distraction from your days:

Get less email.

You're probably saying to yourself right now, "Yeah, sure, I'll get right on that. Let me practice mind-melding with everyone on Earth to persuade them to stop sending me email."

But seriously, you have more control than you think over how much email lands in your inbox. Try these tactics for starters:

Unsubscribe

Hit that little *unsubscribe* link at the bottom of every newsletter and email list, except for the ones you actually read and enjoy. A few months ago I went on an unsubscribing binge, and ended up with just three subscriptions that made the cut. Also, when you land on an email list because you bought something from someone, unsubscribe as soon as you receive that first email. It seems easier to just hit *delete*, but in the long run, you'll save more time and energy if you take a few extra seconds to unsubscribe for good.

Go Incognito

Remove your email address from public websites, your social media accounts, and so on. If your email isn't easy to find, many prospective emailers will move on to people who are easier to contact.

Create a Filter

Email is so easy that many people will send you a message, not because they truly need something from you, but because it's quicker to drop the question into your lap than it is to search Google for the answer. I've actually had people email me questions like, "What's a query letter?" Are they for real? This happens especially to businesspeople, subject matter experts, authors, and other pros with an online presence.

One solution is to make people who want to email you go through a filter to make sure they're serious before they reach out to you. You might require that people wishing to contact you read a FAQ first, and email only if their question isn't answered there, or require them to snail mail you, or mention on your Contact Me page that if someone has a question, you're happy to set up a consulting call at a rate of $X per hour. If they pay up, you'll know they *really* wanted to talk to you.

Use a Throwaway Address

Create a new email address on a free service like Gmail or Hotmail that you can use if you absolutely must enter your email into a form to get something you want. I have such an address on Hotmail, which I check every few months. That inbox is full of nothing but hot, steaming junk.

You can also use a service like Sneakemail.com, which lets you create unlimited disposable email addresses for $2 per month.

Refuse to Give It Up

You know how you can't buy something in a store these days without the cashier asking for your email address, phone number, blood type, and mother's maiden name before they ring you up? It completely baffles me when I see people quietly comply, as if it's a prerequisite to the store taking their money. *You can say no!* I simply say, "I prefer not to share my email," and the cashier hits some magical button that skips that page. If you want to receive emails from that store, sure (and you can always use your throwaway address)...but otherwise, your email address is private information that retailers don't have a right to.

Use Different Addresses

Creating a new email address is easy, and often free, so it's worth it to have several. You can create different addresses for work, friends, and the public, and check them at varying intervals, depending on the importance of their contents.

For example, I used to have students in my Write for Magazines e-course send their questions and assignments to my primary email address. I was answering student emails every day, at all times of the day and night. If a student email came in while I was in the middle of working on an article assignment, I would drop the assignment and answer the email. Working on a pitch? The email took precedence. Taking a well-deserved lunch break? You guessed it.

When I received a chastising email from a student because I didn't respond to her assignment within 30 minutes, I decided to stop the madness. My life coach suggested I create a separate email address just for student email, and check it only a couple days per week. I followed her advice with my next class, and...success! I make it clear in my course emails and the course FAQ that this is my schedule, so all my students are on board with it and haven't complained.

Once you've put the kibosh on unnecessary emails flooding your inbox, decide what to do with the rest. These three rules for email, which I developed last year—the year I accomplished more than I ever have—will help you reduce the distraction of email without guilt, so you have more time, focus, and energy to kick major butt at your D-I-A Plan.

Rule #1. *People Can Wait*

Just because people can email you quickly doesn't mean you have to respond quickly. You set your priorities for the day, and sometimes that means the people emailing you will have to wait. If you're following a D-I-A Plan, that takes precedence over the (often imagined) wants and needs of other people—especially people you don't know.

Many emailers don't consider that everyone has stuff in their life, and that just like them, the people they're emailing have a lot going on. If you're following a D-I-A Plan, that goes double for you. Take one typical week I experienced last March: My husband was in Tokyo all week, and our son had three-hour ballet rehearsals almost every evening. At the end of that week, we had a guest, and then spent an entire Saturday at the theater for the two dance recitals. On top of that, my business partner and I were launching a new class, and we spent many hours that week working with our team to make the class a reality.

Do you think I responded to every email within minutes, or even hours, that week? No, it was more like days, and a few responses took weeks.

Stuff happens. People understand that. If they don't, then they need to. You can always set an autoresponder, letting emailers know you're underwater and will be slow in getting back to them. Heck, you can make that autoresponder permanent!

Rule #2. *Not Every Person Needs (or Deserves) a Response*

Emails come from real, living humans, and real, living humans deserve your respect. But that doesn't mean every person deserves a *response*. If you're walking down the street and a gang of construction workers catcalls you, do you feel bad for giving them the side-eye as you walk on by?

If it's clear someone is wasting your time, like by asking you to share an infographic on your blog that has nothing to do with your niche, or is baiting you for a fight, or is in a tizzy over a typo, then no response is needed.

For example, a member of my mailing list responded to my Monday Motivation email today with nothing but a single link. When I clicked on it, it took me to an Amazon page listing his novels. Do you think I responded to that?

As another example, marketing emails and newsletters obviously don't require a response, unless you really feel moved to say something. I have some people on my mailing list who immediately respond to every Monday Motivation email I send out. It's sweet, and I appreciate the thought and effort, but I also wonder how much work those writers are getting done.

Finally, a situation will often resolve itself if you just wait it out. ("Never mind, I figured it out on my own/found it on my hard drive/

found someone else to answer the question.") Hold off on answering instead of jumping right on the situation, and you may *never* have to respond.

Rule #3. *If It's That Important, They'll Come Back*

As the News Editor at BoardGameGeek.com, my husband gets a ton of email. He's had upwards of 1,300 emails in his inbox at one time. I keep trying to get him to simply delete all the emails he is obviously never going to be able to get to.

Here's why: If an email is important, and absolutely requires a response or an action on your part, the sender will follow up.

No one wants to declare email bankruptcy, but sometimes it's the kindest thing you can do for yourself. Yes, emails come from real, live people you want to be nice to—but if you're overloaded with emails you'll never have the time to respond to, you're only stressing yourself out and creating a guilt complex every time you open your inbox.

If it gets to this point, delete all the emails in your inbox, and you'll discover many of these people didn't need you after all.

My challenge to you: Put some of these tips into place right now so you can start getting less email, and use the saved time to do whatever it takes to build a full, fun D-I-A life.

Chapter 22

Kill Your TV

I know people who get home from work and plop down in front of the TV until bedtime. Then they complain not only about not having enough time to do it all, but about being too exhausted to do *anything*!

TV can suck up both your time and energy, and if you're going to lead an amazing D-I-A life, you'll need plenty of both. I understand that after a hard day at work, taking care of your family, or going to school, you deserve to relax. But TV is not so much relaxing as draining. Sure, following one or two programs can add some harmless fun to your week, but if you have the boob tube on all evening like the average American, perhaps it's time to rethink how you're spending your hours.

Here's how to drop the TV habit. And if YouTube, Netflix, or random online surfing are your time-sucks of choice, many of these tips will work for those, too.

Replace It

Yes, of course you deserve to relax and have a good time, especially after a long day. But what if, instead of watching TV, you find an option for relaxing that's more in line with your current D-I-A Desire? For example, for the D-I-A Desire *Gain Mad Skills*, read a book about the new skill you're working on. For *Travel*, hold a family meeting to work out plans for a cruise. And for *Grow Your Spiritual Practice*, you can meditate, journal, or pray. These activities not only take less time than a typical TV program, and get you closer to your D-I-A Desires, but they leave you feeling refreshed and motivated, as well—the opposite of the way you feel after watching an *America's Next Top Model* marathon.

Cut the Cable

Would you watch less TV if you didn't have 200+ channels to choose from? Then gain time, boost your energy, and save money by dropping your cable subscription.

Unplug

Doing something as simple as unplugging your TV can help you cut down on tube-viewing hours. If you have to plug it in before watching, you'll have a moment of space to consider whether you'd rather do something more productive and energizing.

Go Cold Turkey

Stash your TV in a closet—unless you have the kind that's attached to the wall, in which case you can throw a blanket over it. Eventually, if you find you don't have the urge to watch it at all anymore, you can sell it. This may sound extreme, but I know plenty of people who live TV-free. You can find lots of other more important things to occupy your time, like your D-I-A Plan!

Set a Timer

Can't go cold turkey? Set a kitchen timer for a little less time than you usually spend watching TV in the evening, and shave off 15 more minutes each day. When the buzzer sounds, turn off the TV and find something else to do.

Multi-Task

If you have a show you absolutely have to watch, try performing tasks that don't take up much of your attention while you indulge, like folding laundry, running on a treadmill, or addressing holiday cards. For example, people always ask my friend and business partner Diana the secret of her knitting productivity. Her answer is that she cannot watch her TV programs without knitting at the same time. When her show is over, she turns off the TV and puts down the needles.

Here's my little secret: We have one show we just *have* to watch—*Project Runway*—and our son has become a movie buff, as well. So we watch TV and movies while we eat dinner.

I can hear your gasps. I was even lectured once by a friend who reported breathlessly that it's terrible for your family to eat in front of the TV because you don't socialize while you eat, you gain weight from eating mindlessly, and add-scary-statistic-here. Well, maybe it's terrible for *her* family, but we have plenty of other time for chatting and playing due to our work schedules, and we're all at a healthy weight. So as with anything else, decide what's right for *you*.

Anything you simply *look at*, like TV and YouTube, steal time from activities that will bring you energy, joy, and cherished memories. Why get sucked into music videos on YouTube when you can learn to play an instrument? Why watch a sport on TV when you can play it yourself? Why surf Upworthy for heartwarming stories when you can create them in your own life?

Stop passively watching and start actively doing—that's what the D-I-A life is all about.

Chapter 23

Sleep Less

How much more could you accomplish if you magically had an extra hour in the day? Well, you can make this magic hour happen—by sleeping less.

You may huff, "I don't get enough sleep as it is! Don't you know we're a chronically underslept nation?" If you were to pick up any form of media directed at women, you would believe we're so busy that we don't even log enough Z's to remain upright during the day.

And yet, in 2014 the American Time Use Survey showed that on average, we're sleeping 8.76 hours per day. That sure does sound like a lot of snooze time! In fact, for some people, it may be too much snooze time. Sleeping *less* may make you *more* productive.

A study in the journal *Sleep* concluded: "Only shorter than average sleepers (<7.5 h) spent more time socializing, relaxing, and engaging in leisure activities, while both short (<5.5 h) and long sleepers (≥8.5 h) watched more TV than the average sleeper."

In other words, people who slept between 5.5 and 7.5 hours per night spent more time doing more stuff.

Everyone's sleep needs are different. But if you're one of those people who can get by on less sleep than average, wouldn't you like to use those hours to go after your D-I-A Desires? Imagine you're one of the lucky ones who can feel great and maintain good health with just six hours of slumber: What could you do with almost three extra hours every single day compared to the average sleeper?

Go Slow

I suggest experimenting with your sleep time to see how much you really need, instead of simply going along with how long your body wants to lounge in bed because you're feeling lazy, unmotivated, or anxious about the coming day. Try cutting back on your sleep by 15 minutes every few days. When you get to the point where you're feeling sleepy during the day, bump your sleep time back up by 15 minutes and keep it there.

If I let myself sleep as long as I want, I usually clock in at around 8.5 hours, but I know from experimenting that I still feel great with just seven hours. Any less than that and you won't want to be around me.

Important note: *You don't have to get up early.* I know every personal development book and blog post in the known universe says only total losers sleep past 5 am, and that people who go to bed at 1 am are either lazy or workaholics. Well, I say we D-I-A women all need to do what's right for *us*. If you're a night owl, try staying up a little later every night until you feel tired the next day, then move your bedtime back a bit.

Force Your Hand

When I decide I need more morning hours to work on my D-I-A Desires, I simply start setting the alarm for 5 am or earlier. When the alarm goes off, I suck it up and get out of bed, no matter how much I'd rather doze another hour or two. Many of us find it difficult to go to bed earlier than normal when we plan to rise early, and this method forces your hand: Within a day or two, you'll be tired enough that you'll naturally want to hit the sack earlier, and rising early won't be as difficult. If you tend to hit the *Sleep* button multiple times, try putting the alarm clock across the room so you'll have to get up to turn it off.

Sleep Better

Improve the quality of your sleep, and you'll need less of it. We've all heard about sleep hygiene habits like keeping your bedroom dark, cool, and quiet, and not drinking caffeine after noon. If you haven't adopted these basics, please do so. Invest in blackout shades, or even throw a blanket over the curtain rods if your room tends to be too light, and download a free white noise app for your phone if the room is too noisy. The typical temperature recommendation for primo sleep is between 65° and 72°, so experiment with your thermostat to see what temperature helps you snooze better and wake up less frequently during the night.

Other, less well-known, sleep hygiene habits include: Go to sleep before 11 pm to avoid the hit of adrenaline that can keep you awake all night; avoid alcohol, which fractures your sleep; and turn off all screens a couple hours before your bedtime, since the light can keep you from becoming drowsy. If you must work late, you can try a screen dimmer app like f.lux that will let you work into the night without suffering from the glare of the screen.

Hack Your Sleep

Many intrepid experimenters are working on sleep hacks that dramatically boost sleep quality so you can get by with less. For example, I take magnesium before bed, and other people swear by melatonin, fish oil, and other supplements. Google *sleep hacks* and you'll find dozens of ideas to try.

Get Grounded

I thought grounding (aka earthing) sounded wacky and woo-woo when I first heard about it, but being a bit wacky and woo-woo myself, I decided to try it. The theory is that our bodies are meant to come into contact with a grounding force—that is, the Earth—regularly, because the Earth has a negative charge that balances out the positive charge our bodies build up from living in the modern, electrified world. Proponents say grounding helps us sleep better, reduce stress, increase energy, and even beat insomnia.

You can buy all sorts of gadgets like earthing mats and earthing sheets, which are convenient. Or you can just go outside and stand barefoot on the ground. When I was overwhelmed with jet lag after a recent trip, I went out and stood on our cold lawn in bare feet for about

15 minutes, then went to bed. It busted that heavy jet lag fast when nothing else had worked.

Make a Movie

You want to get up in the wee hours to have more time for your D-I-A Plan, but when you hit the sack at night you spend an hour tossing and turning. That stinks, because a good rest will help you gather energy for the next busy day. Luckily, I have a trick to get you to sleep within ten minutes. I trained our son to use this technique, and it works for him, too!

Imagine the day you just had. But don't just mull over your day—imagine it in real-time, like you're watching a movie of your day. See yourself getting up and splashing water on your face. Imagine how you went downstairs, and every step of preparing your pot of coffee. Then imagine yourself pouring in the milk, stirring the coffee, and drinking it. Don't rush...imagine every aspect as if you were really there right now. How does the water feel? How does the coffee smell?

In most cases, you'll be asleep before you even get to drinking the coffee. Forcing yourself to imagine each minute of your day calms your mind and keeps distracting thoughts from creeping in.

Empty Your Brain

Another way to fall asleep faster is to write down everything that's on your mind right before you turn in, so you don't have to contend with your brain shouting, "Hey, don't fall asleep yet…I want to think about that exam we have tomorrow! Oh, and you forgot to call the repairman!" I included a Night-Time Brain Dump Worksheet in the downloadable bonus package just for this purpose.

Create a Morning Routine You Love

You want to get up early, but it's *so hard*. One of the reasons we hate to rise early is that we're not looking forward to what awaits us when we do get up: Maybe you're dealing with kid squabbles as they get ready for school, preparing school lunches, getting ready for work, and then heading to a soul-sucking job. Or maybe you don't have a job and you want one, and are looking ahead to another day of sending out resumes and crossing your fingers. Whatever the reasons, the coming 24 hours are not looking awesome.

If I were to wake up at my body's normal time—usually around 7:30 am—I would come downstairs to a little boy who immediately needed something: A cup of tea, a blanket, entertainment. I love my kid to the moon and back, but having to be *on* the instant I crawl out of bed, and needing to react immediately to other people's needs, is a bummer of a way to start the day.

But when I get up at 5 am, I'm guaranteed time to myself to read, sip tea, listen to motivational podcasts, meditate, write in my journal, and work on my D-I-A Desires. By the time the kid gets up, I'm ready to be *on* for the day. This solitary, quiet time becomes one of the best parts of the day, and knowing I'll have it makes waking up in the wee hours much easier.

What can you do in the morning that will make waking up early feel like a reward, so you have more hours in the day for your D-I-A Desires? Here are some ideas:

- Journal.
- Meditate.
- Go out for a walk or a run.
- Do yoga.
- Listen to music.
- Sip tea or coffee.
- Write out your plan for the day.
- Listen to a podcast.
- Read a novel or a personal development book.
- Take a bath or a long shower.
- Use a foam roller or tennis ball to massage the kinks out of your back and shoulders.

If you get up two hours earlier than usual, even if you spend 30 minutes easing into the day in a pleasurable way, that leaves 90 minutes free for pursuing your D-I-A Plan.

Of course, our first instinct after slapping off the alarm is to jump into essential, un-fun tasks, which defeats the purpose of rising early. Here are some morning to-don'ts, if you want to wake up looking forward to the day:

- Don't check email (Does anyone really need a response at 5 am?).
- Don't login to Facebook, Twitter, Instagram, or whatever. When you do, you're waking up to other people's problems, needs, and goals…yuck!
- Don't jump right into work (unless you're doing it out of inspiration and not pressure).
- Don't look at the news (I can't think of more of a kill-joy way to wake up to the day).

Whatever you do when you rise early should make you feel amazing, so that you'll keep wanting to do it.

Wake Up and Get Moving

You're convinced you can do more amazing stuff by sleeping less, and it's been going great…until today. You went to bed early, set your alarm for some ridiculously early hour, had a fabulous morning routine—or you worked late on a D-I-A Desire, and now it's time to get ready for your actual paying work—and you just can't seem to wake up. Ugh.

Some days you can't get going, and you drag all morning. Even your usual cup of java doesn't have its usual effect. For the woman who wants to do it all, a lack of energy and motivation in the morning is a major roadblock.

Sometimes you just need to pull back and relax. No matter how ambitious you are or how many goals you have in your D-I-A Plan, you simply can't go full-throttle day after day without a break. So if your mind and body are crying for rest, do it however you can.

But sometimes, you're feeling *blah* for no reason, and need to get your mojo back fast so you can get on with your D-I-A Plan. When that happens, here's a whole arsenal of tricks you can use to wake yourself up and boost your energy so you can sail through the day.

Drink Up

At night you go hours without drinking, and the resulting dehydration can cause you to feel sluggish when you get up. Try quaffing a full glass of water spiked with lemon or lime for a quick pick-me-up as soon as you rise. In fact, I like to keep a glass of water on the bookshelf in our bedroom so I can grab it after I stumble out of bed.

Brush Up

No, I don't mean to brush your teeth, though you should definitely do that every morning. I mean dry brushing, which is gently brushing your skin in the direction of your heart with a dry natural-bristle brush. This is incredibly rejuvenating in the morning, and it takes only a couple of minutes. (It also makes your skin look amazing.)

Step Out

A dose of sunlight tells your body it's time to wake up, so throw open the curtains as soon as you rise. If you can, go outside for a minute or two, even if it's just to get the mail. In warm weather, I like to spend time on my screened-in porch with a cup of tea, soaking in the sun. If you tend to be more draggy in the winter, consider investing in a light box; all you have to do is sit in front of it for about half an hour each morning during the cold, dark season to help beat the winter *blahs*. A good light box costs around $200; mine was from Northern Light Technologies. Although they're not quite the same, you can also find free light alarm mobile apps that gradually brighten your bedroom when it's time to wake up.

Move It

As we discussed in Chapter 10, *Take the Drug*, exercise gives you both time and energy. A walk, a stretching routine, or a few yoga moves can take you from *no go* to *go go* in 20 minutes. Some yoga studios offer early-morning classes, or you can use one of the many free videos on YouTube. Another option is to hire a personal trainer to come to your home early in the morning a few days a week to give you a workout.

Chill Out

In his book *The 7 Day Energy Surge*, Jim Karas recommends taking a cold shower in the morning to boost your energy all day. I'm not brave or crazy enough to jump straight into a freezing shower; I take my usual warm shower, and then at the end I turn the water to as cold as I can stand for a couple of minutes. Studies show it can help you lose weight, too!

What to Do if You Still Feel Terrible

If you're practicing good sleep hygiene, are getting a normal amount of sleep, and have a morning routine designed to boost your energy, but you still feel tired and unmotivated all day, please see a medical professional. You may be depressed, have sleep apnea, or be suffering from another medical issue that's draining your energy. One of my family members underwent a sleep study, and the technicians reported she stopped breathing 50 times an hour! Another friend did a sleep study and discovered she was having seizures all night long, so she was getting only 60% of the sleep she needed, despite sleeping ten hours per night. Medical problems like these can be keeping you down, even if you don't know they're happening.

Chapter 24

Have an Agenda

I once coached a magazine writer who had few chunks of time during the day that were long enough to train for a 5k. She'd have a few minutes here and a few minutes there, but no stretches of 60 minutes, or even 30 minutes, to train hard toward her goal.

After asking some questions, I noticed my client was letting her expert sources choose the times and days for their interviews, so she would have calls scattered throughout the day—a perfect recipe for feeling like you have no time, even when you really do if you were to add it all up. You can get tons done in short spurts of time, but it certainly is a handy excuse to go down a rabbit hole of clickbait articles instead.

If my wellness coaching client wanted time to train for that 5k, she would need to find a way to batch all her interviews together so she'd have a chunk of open time instead of a bunch of 15-minute blocks sprinkled throughout the day.

I used to have the same issue. When I gave away 50 free wellness coaching calls to build my business, at first I asked prospective coachees to send me a few days and times that worked for them, and I would choose from these. But letting other people control my schedule resulted in chaos, and I didn't have enough solid blocks of time to pursue my other goals.

So I started offering coachees one choice: "Would you be available on Monday at 11 am?" Usually they said yes, but if it didn't work for them, I would offer another option. The result: I was scheduling coaching sessions in one chunk of the day, with short breaks in between to let me use the bathroom or get a cup of tea. Then, later in the day I had loads of time to work on my other goals. My writer client tried the same tactic, and was able to create big enough chunks of time to train for her 5k.

Pursuing your D-I-A Plan requires solid blocks of time—to volunteer, meditate, study, entertain, read, or whatever—which means taking command of your schedule is über important. If you let other people control your schedule and try to fit your D-I-A Plan into the time that's left over, chances are you'll never get to work on your Goals at all, and will wake up one day when you're 85, wondering where the time went and why you never did what you really wanted to.

If you let other people set your deadlines, say yes to everything that comes your way, and jump every time someone breathlessly approaches you with another fire to put out, you'll soon find yourself living other people's visions instead of your own. One thing I've learned from experience is this: If you don't set your own agenda, other people will be only too glad to set it for you.

Here are some other ways you can control your agenda, and become the master of your fate and captain of your soul:

Decide What's Important

Schedule blocks of time in your calendar for your D-I-A Desires, and then fit in other to-dos around those blocks.

Act in Advance

Set up appointments well ahead of time so you have a better choice of time slots. For example, if your dog's annual checkup is normally in June, schedule it in March. If you wait until a week before your pup is due for his checkup, you'll likely have to accept an appointment time that's not the most convenient for you.

Schedule Standing Appointments

In the example above, an even better idea would be to schedule standing appointments, if the vet allows it. For example, your dog is scheduled for a checkup every first Monday in June at 8 am. You get your hair cut and colored every eighth Saturday at 5 pm. Your kids have a standing appointment at the dentist the first Mondays of September and March, right after school. You get the idea!

Negotiate

Sometimes you'll hear from a service provider that they're available at X date and time. For example, the appliance repairman will stop by between 12 and 4 pm tomorrow, or your new furniture will arrive on Friday at 11 am. You don't have to accept the first time they offer you. That's the time that's most convenient to *them*, but if it doesn't work for *you*, see if you can get an appointment that will mesh better with your schedule. Sometimes you'll have to wait a little longer, but if there's no real rush, it makes sense to reschedule.

You can also negotiate deadlines. For example, as a journalist, I used to accept every magazine assignment, no matter what the deadline was, and then I'd find myself with four articles due in one week and zero in the following three weeks. After years of this crazy-making cycle, I finally smartened up and started asking editors for different deadline dates—sometimes earlier, sometimes later—so the flow of work was more even. I'd tell my editors, "I already have an assignment due that week, and want to make sure I have the time and focus to do a great job on yours. Could I turn it in the following week?" When you couch your request in terms of benefits to your client or employer, they're more likely to agree.

Schedule Your Fun

I like to chat with friends on the phone. Often, someone will call to shoot the breeze and I'll just pick up and go with it. But when I have a lot going on, we'll actually schedule our BS session at a time that works for both of us. The same concept would work for FaceTime talks with your college kids and Skyping with your parents. It seems kind of stick-up-the-butt to schedule chats with your loved ones like a business consultant, but people generally don't mind, and you can then work on doing it all without interruptions from your phone. Movie dates, coffee with friends, and hikes with your partner can also be scheduled so they'll fit into your D-I-A life—and so you don't fall into the trap of always saying, "We *really* need to get together for coffee sometime."

Block Them

If someone is bugging you, kick them out of your life. For example, I know people who will get a call, look at their phone, and say, "I recognize that number...it's the foghorn phone spammer again." And then they'll ignore it. Why not block the number? Same with email: If you're being bugged or harassed by someone and can't get them to stop, use your email system's blacklist feature to block them for good. While it may seem easier to ignore the interruptions, every time it happens you're distracted and have to spend time getting back on task.

You can also block all *unknown* callers, which is callers who block their caller ID so you can't tell who they are. The blocking methods depend on the type of phone you have. Android and iPhone have apps that will let you do this, as well, like the highly rated Mr. Number app. If someone doesn't want to reveal their number or location, chances are you don't want to talk with them. You're way too busy creating an awesome, D-I-A life to deal with interruptions from spammers and telemarketers!

Develop Attitude

I love that poster you see in offices that says, "Lack of planning on your part does not constitute an emergency on mine." That's the attitude to develop if you're to create a D-I-A life. Remember, you want to live your vision, not ignore your Goals to put out someone else's fires. You can delegate the issue to someone else, schedule a better time to tackle it, or simply delete it from your life if you dare; as I mentioned in Chapter 21, *Stop Checking Your Email*, many problems resolve themselves if you just leave them alone. I can't count how many times I've gotten an email from someone who is freaking out over something, and 30 minutes later they email back and say, "Never mind."

Don't worry...people won't be offended if you're firm about what you can do and when you can do it. They'll understand, and even admire you, if you say you don't work on weekends, your planning time is sacred, or you can't babysit their two charming children because that's the time you work on building your side business.

Develop your own agenda and stick to it, instead of letting other people control your time. It's the only way to lead a creative, full, D-I-A life.

Chapter 25

Do Things Out of Order

We do certain things at certain times, right? The order must never vary: We get up, work out at the gym, shower, go to work for eight hours, commute home, eat dinner, socialize or relax, and save chores, errands, and fun for the weekends.

But this schedule leaves very little time for getting out there and kicking major D-I-A butt. In fact, it takes up the entire day, from early in the morning until bedtime. Why do we adhere to a schedule that doesn't give us time to live an awesome, outstanding, exciting life? It's because we develop habits so that we don't need to analyze every single decision. If we do the same things the same way every day, that conserves our mental brainpower for other things.

However, our habits can lead us astray. It's easy and efficient to do the same things the same way every day, but not if our habits themselves are inefficient. Yes, it takes mental effort to rethink our schedules and the time-worn, comfy way we go through our days. But examining our habits will help us save time and energy in the long run.

To create a D-I-A life, we need time and energy, but the typical schedule is very good at draining both. So my challenge to you is to make a list of everything you do in a day, from brewing your morning coffee to brushing your teeth before bed, and then go over the list and analyze each item. Does this task need to be done at the time you normally do it? Does it have to take as much time as it normally does? Do you have to do it at all?

Some examples:

The 8-Hour Work Day

To paraphrase Tim Ferriss in his book *The 4-Hour Workweek*, isn't it amazing that every job takes exactly eight hours per day, five days per week to accomplish? Instead, can you talk your boss into a more flexible schedule? Or maybe you can focus intently and get all your work done in four hours, and use the other four hours to pursue your D-I-A Goals?

I've read case studies of employees who were able to show their bosses they could get all their expected work done, and then some—and offer more value to the company than other workers—in fewer than 40 hours per week. The employees would then negotiate a shorter workday or workweek.

To pull this off, you would need to show your employer exactly how much value you add to the company's bottom line, because if your main argument is that it doesn't take you eight hours to get your work done, you may find yourself busted down to part-time wages. Your goal is to work less, but earn the same amount of money, and employers (if they're smart) are shelling out for value, not hours. Of course, use this strategy at your discretion, as only you can tell if your employer is the type that would be open to the suggestion.

If you're a free agent, it's always within your rights to cut down your work hours if you can serve your clients and keep them happy while working less.

The Morning Shower

Does everyone need to shower every day? Maybe you have a dirty job, or you sweat it out at the gym every morning. And sometimes there's nothing better than taking a hot shower for no reason at all. But for many of us, there are only a few parts of the body that need daily cleansing, and those parts make up a pretty small percentage of our body. Not only that, but more and more dermatologists and hairdressers are saying that daily bathing and shampooing are *bad* for your skin and hair! So why spend an hour every day bathing your entire body, applying six kinds of lotion to recover from the drying effects of the shower, slathering in your multiple hair products—which you just washed out of your hair five minutes ago—and re-styling your hair?

Here's a little secret: I shower every other day. The odd days = a washcloth and dry shampoo. Maybe a flatiron if I wake up with my hair looking like one of those troll dolls. On shower days, I give myself the works: I scrub the heck out of my skin with a body brush, shave, and use a foot file.

If you insist on remaining a daily shower devotee, would showering before bed instead of in the morning free up the most productive part of your day? If you work at home, could you shower during the afternoon, when your energy is lower and you're not doing your best work anyway? As a bonus, the shower might wake you up!

The Morning Run

Sure, all the health pundits tell us the best time to exercise is before work, and an hour-long run is the typical go-to for a morning workout. But keep in mind these health pundits are sometimes writers who are interviewing the same old sources and spouting the party line, despite being couch spuds themselves. An embarrassing example: I once wrote a nutrition article for a newsstand health magazine while consuming an entire brick of cream cheese. Also, the experts don't know us. Maybe it works better for you to train for your 5k at 3 am, and then nap at your desk during lunch. No judging here...we're all different people.

Some other options:

- Hire an in-home personal trainer to come to your office at lunchtime.
- Divide up your exercise routine into ten-minute chunks and scatter them throughout the work day.
- Try High Intensity Interval Training (HIIT), which is intense workouts that can be as short as four minutes.
- Exercise before bed. You've probably also heard that you shouldn't exercise within two hours before bedtime because it can keep you from falling asleep. But why not try it out to see if that's true for *your* schedule and physiology? If the best time

for you to work up a sweat is 9 pm, and you fall asleep just fine, who cares what the experts say?

My point is that no one knows your body and your schedule like you do. Instead of going with the same-old-same-old exercise schedule regime it's what everyone else says is right, think about whether mixing things up will help you in your quest to do it all.

The Evening Dinner Rush

Typical after-work hours look like some variation of this: You get home, decide what to have for dinner, then realize you're missing a key ingredient for the meal you suddenly really, really want. You or your partner run to the store and grab the missing ingredient, even though your fridge is full of other options. Then you cook, set the table, eat, and clean up—which often takes more time than the eating. Now you're exhausted and ready to relax until bedtime. No one questions this.

But what if you analyzed your dinner-making process and figured out a way to streamline it? For example, you could:

1. Plan meals a week in advance, buy all the ingredients using your grocery store's online shopping service, and stick to the plan come hell or high water.
2. Make recipes you can double and eat two days in a row.
3. Spend a weekend with a friend making a load of freezer meals, so you don't have to cook again for a couple of weeks.
4. Schedule one day per week where the kids plan and prepare dinner.
5. Opt for one-pot meals that are easy to cook and clean up.
6. Use the slow cooker you've had in your cabinet for years. Throw in the ingredients in the morning, so when you get home a hot meal is waiting for you.
7. Sign up for a meal delivery service.
8. Plan for meals with easy prep, but long cooking time. For example, you could roast a chicken, turkey breast, or cut of beef or pork; partway through the cooking time, throw some

potatoes in the oven to bake as well. You'll then have plenty of time to work on your current D-I-A Desire while dinner pretty much makes itself.

9. Order in pizza once a week and used the saved time to work on your D-I-A Desire.
10. Trade off with your partner: One of you cooks, the other cleans up afterward.

You could also try a combo of tactics: For example, I always do #1, #2, and #10, and often combine these with #6 and #8. So on Friday I'll create a meal plan and shop online, and on Monday I'll make a double batch of chicken soup in the slow cooker. All I have to do is toss the ingredients into the slow cooker (including a whole chicken…no need to even cut it up), turn the cooker on, and in eight hours dinner is served—for two days. That adds up to a lot of time and energy saved for higher-priority projects.

Want to change up your schedule to get more done? The 9 to 5 office schedule I'm ragging on here is typical of many people, but it may not resonate with you. You can use the same process—list, analyze, change—even if you work nights, are a stay-at-home mom, take care of your aging parents, and so on. The thoughts in this chapter are just to give you an idea of how the process works. Now, try it with your daily schedule and see what happens. I wager you'll find many ways to be more efficient as you go through your day, which not only saves time and energy, but is highly motivational as well.

Chapter 26

Schedule an Admin Day

My friend Aleks told me about this meme that was floating around the internet a while back: "Man, if you wanna know what a woman's mind feels like, imagine a browser with 2,857 tabs open. All. The. Time."

Our minds are a maelstrom of to-dos. "The car needs an oil change. The cats are overdue for their flea medication. We're in charge of snacks at our kid's school next week. Argh!" It's hard to work on a D-I-A Plan when so many tasks are whirling around in our heads like highly caffeinated toddlers. We want to get them done *right now*, just to get them off our plates—to the detriment of our *big* Goals.

Years ago, I learned about the concept of Admin Days from the book *Work Less, Make More* by Jennifer White.

You set aside an Admin Day specifically for taking care of the little things in life that may not be essential to your D-I-A Desires, but need to get done nonetheless. Some small tasks you may be able to automate, and some you may be able to hire out—but some you know you'll just have to suck it up and take care of.

Having all these little duties, tasks, mini-quests, projects, errands, assignments—whatever you want to call them—floating around in your consciousness distracts you from your D-I-A Desires, and setting a regular Admin Day will help you clear them out of your brain. Schedule a whole day, or several hours on one or more days during the week, depending on your schedule. You can use this time to accomplish things like:

- Answering non-essential emails.
- Updating your computer's or phone's operating system, WordPress plugins, software, apps, etc.
- Wrapping gifts.
- Writing thank-you notes.
- Planning meals.
- Doing small repairs.
- RSVPing to invitations.
- Making non-essential calls.
- Clipping coupons/checking deal sites/updating your savings apps like Cartwheel/etc.
- Making a trip to the post office.
- Listing items for sale on Craigslist, eBay, etc.
- Making store returns.
- Dropping off/picking up dry cleaning.
- Ordering prescription refills.
- Paying bills.
- Watering indoor plants.
- Taking stock of your pantry for your next shopping trip.
- Sketching out your schedule for the following week.
- Changing HVAC filters.
- Ordering flowers for Mother's Day.

Here's an example of my Admin Day list for this week:

- Start the tax packet for our accountant.
- Answer emails.
- Transfer money from PayPal to our bank account.
- Install the BB8 nightlight in our son's room.
- Add our son's 2016-17 school events to our calendar (start of school, teacher work days, etc.).
- Install new door.
- Plan school snacks for next week.
- Order groceries.
- Fill out and send in school re-enrollment form.
- Supervise writing of thank-you notes.

- Ask D about whether there's a way to darken the portrait I drew.
- Sort mail.
- Pay bills.

Normally, those tasks would be eating at me until I sucked it up, abandoned my more important projects, and cleared them off my list. But now, I know I'll get to them all on my Admin Day on Friday, so they're off my mind and I can focus on my D-I-A Goals Monday through Thursday. There aren't many tasks that can't wait a few days to get done.

Want to save your time and energy for the things that matter most—like your D-I-A Plan? Here's an assignment: Figure out what day would work best for you as an Admin Day. If you work 9-5 during the week, you may want to use half of Saturday to take care of the tasks that build up during the week. If you work at home, you could set aside one full day, as I do, as an Admin Day. Then use the Admin Day To-Do List that's included as one of the free downloadable worksheets you get with this book, and start adding items to it as they come up.

Whatever you do, don't make the mistake of scheduling a little time every day to take care of projects from your Admin Day list. To ditch that scattered feeling you get when you have a hundred things vying for real estate in your brain, you truly need one big chunk of time— at least half a day—where you know you can focus on the tasks and bang through them all at once. Also, don't over-analyze your to-dos: Throw anything onto the list you're fairly sure can wait a few days without the world ending.

Afraid to push off all your to-dos to one day per week? Try using an Admin Day just a few times, and I guarantee you'll soon realize the world won't spin off its axis if you don't attend to things the instant they enter your consciousness.

Chapter 27

Put It on Auto

One powerful way to make time for your D-I-A Desires is to automate as much of the process as you can. In fact, it's a good idea to automate *everything* that's automatable, whether or not it has to do with your D-I-A Plan.

When you automate an action, you only have to muster up the willpower to think about it once, and then it keeps rolling along on its own. For example:

Automate Your Reminders

Remember that quote about women having 2,857 tabs open in their mental browsers? Well, instead of having tabs eternally open, you could schedule reminders and then close those tabs until you need them.

For example, for years I've been using the free service MemoToMe.com to email me reminders a week before my loved ones' birthdays. I included their addresses in the reminders so I can send them a card without having to dig up their info. Look up *free reminder service* online and you'll find plenty more, including reminder apps for your phone.

I also put *everything* in my calendar and set up the events to ding my husband and me via pop-up the day before. So every month on the 10th we get a pop-up reminding us that the cats get their flea treatment the next day. Every month on the 24th, a pop-up reminds us that the next day we need to change the HVAC filters. Twice a year we get dinged about oil changes for the cars. And so on.

Automate Your Appointments

We talked about this earlier: Set regular, ongoing appointments with the doctor, dentist, vet, eye doctor, accountant, hairdresser, and so on, so you never have to think about these things again.

Automate Your Help

As we discussed in Chapter 18, *Get Support*, paying people to do what you don't want to do, and to help you reach your D-I-A Desires, can save you loads of time, energy, and even money. And when you automate that help, your goals take care of themselves on autopilot. For example:

- As part of the D-I-A Desire *Create an Amazing Home*, hire cleaners and landscapers to come at the same time every week.
- For the D-I-A Desire *Cross a Finish Line*, hire a trainer to come by every Monday and Thursday at 7 am.
- When you're ready to work on the Desire *Start a Side Hustle*, sign up for a package of sessions with a business coach and schedule them at the same time every week.
- Ready for *Grow Your Spiritual Practice*? Purchase a bunch of sessions with a personal yoga instructor and set a regular day and time for your classes.

Even better, foster self-accountability by pre-paying for your automated help up front. If you bail, you're out money—so you won't bail. For example, last year I wrote one check paying for 30 personal training sessions, and every five weeks I purchase another package of sessions from my yoga instructor. You can probably talk your cleaning company into letting you pre-pay for a month-long (or longer) cleaning package, and so on.

I'm all about low-cost solutions, but it's difficult to automate help you aren't paying for, because the people aren't obligated to help you, and they typically aren't as invested in it. For example, even if you convinced an athletic friend help you train for a marathon *gratis*, you can hardly ask her to commit to training you on a strict schedule for nothing. But again, everyone is different, so if you think of a way to automate unpaid help, or know people who are willing to help you for free on your schedule...by all means!

Automate Your Tasks

Think of all the small tasks you do every day, every week, and every month that you can hand off to automation. For example:

- Sign up for online bill paying wherever you can. It will take some time and effort up front, but you'll never find yourself writing checks for a stack of unpaid bills again.
- Use an app like TextExpander to automate your typing. With this app, you create keystroke shortcuts that will expand into full words, sentences, paragraphs, whatever. For instance, when I type in *bbio*, my entire writing bio pops into the document, and when I type *aaddr*, my home address appears. TextExpander tells me I've saved 110 hours since July 2014. That's one full workweek per year! Another good app is Google Lab's Canned Responses, which lets you answer emails using pre-written responses—perfect if you tend to get the same questions over and over.
- Sign up for a service like Amazon's Subscribe and Save to schedule regular deliveries of items you buy often, such as dog food, diapers, and paper towels. A bonus is that if you purchase a certain amount per month, Amazon will give you a 5% discount.
- Use a service like Carbonite to automatically back up your computer's data at regular intervals. It runs in the background every day and backs up all your data to the cloud, so you don't need to remember to do it.
- Does your business or job require a lot of meetings with clients and prospects? Instead of going back and forth over email for a week to finalize each appointment, try an online scheduler like Acuity Scheduling, Assistant.to (for Gmail), or ScheduleOnce. Set up the dates and times you're available, and your client

or prospect can simply select the time slot they want. Some of these services are free up to a certain number of users or appointments.

Automating tasks like this doesn't only save you time and energy, it also cuts down on the amount of overwhelm in your life and helps you feel less scattered and distracted, simply because you now have that many fewer things to think about. Never again will you think, "Oh man, I need to go to the pet store to get that special dog food for Poochie," or "Jeez, I really need to find time to pay the bills."

Automating your goals and tasks would be a great item for your Admin Day to-do list, so I recommend experimenting with both D-I-A tactics at once.

Chapter 28

Choose Four

Even I will admit that trying to do it all can be overwhelming at times. Some days—or weeks—you feel like a powerhouse of productivity, and make huge strides toward your D-I-A Goals. Other days—or weeks—you feel like you have so much to do, you don't even know where to begin, so you stall out.

If you have trouble getting started on a D-I-A Desire because you have so many things to do you think your head will implode, try the *Rule of Four*:

In the evening before you go to bed, make a list of the four things that must get done the next day in order for you to feel satisfied and productive. These are the four to-dos that will get you closest to your current D-I-A Goal and improve your life in general, *not* the four urgent-but-not-important tasks that are screaming for your attention. In other words, *Answer email* should not be on your list unless it is somehow essential to your Goal.

Jot down short and sweet descriptions; in fact, you should be able to write all four on a Post-It note and stick it to your phone, laptop, mirror, or whatever else you'll see first thing when you wake up. When you get up, look at this teeny, tiny note, breathe a sigh of relief at how short it is, and put your all into those four things before you do anything else that day. Once they're done, you can tackle other projects.

The Rule of Four forces you to prioritize, so you don't end up running around putting out small fires all day, ignoring the embers that are more worthy of your attention. I use this tactic whenever I need it to beat overwhelm, and it helps me focus better when fifty thousand unfinished tasks are zinging around in my brain. My list might look like this:

1. Answer student e-mails.
2. Write one chapter of my book.
3. Schedule family meeting to talk about trip.
4. Sign up our team for the Chocolate 5k.

Four is a doable number, so your resistance to starting is instantly diminished. Imagine telling yourself, "Well, I better get started on those 26 nebulous tasks today," versus, "Wow, I have only these four well-defined goals to meet today, and I'm done!" Which one makes you want to actually start working?

Also, you'll discover that although you built up these tasks to horrific proportions in your mind, once you actually get your butt in gear, you'll finish them fairly quickly—after which you'll be motivated and on a roll. If you choose to tackle more to-dos (remember, you don't have to!), you'll get more done faster. Even if you choose to stop after accomplishing your top four tasks, you should feel pretty good about it because they were your top-priority to-dos, and hopefully this will get you unstuck so you can get back to full-on D-I-A mode the next day.

Check out the Rule of Four Worksheet that's part of your free downloadable bonus package. You may want to use this tactic only when you need it, or you may decide to use it every day, if it helps you get more done than you would without it.

Chapter 29
Hurry Up

When you sort the laundry, can you will your hands to move faster than your usual speed to get the job done more quickly? Yes, you probably can. Can you do your hair more quickly if you will yourself to? I'd say yes. Can you challenge yourself to read faster? Yes indeed.

Many people think the natural speed they happen to work at is simply the best they can do. But, believe it or not, you can make a deliberate decision to move faster when you do anything, including going after your D-I-A Desires. People always say, "I'll get there when I get there!" To which I always want to respond, "Well, you'd get there a lot sooner if you just moved your leg muscles a little faster!"

Many guru-types out there sing the praises of slowing down, but *slow* isn't always the best tactic when you have a whole lot you want to do, and not a lot of time to do it in. Here are some examples of how to put a little boogie in it, to help you live a D-I-A life:

Clean Faster

Let's say you're working on the D-I-A Desire *Create an Amazing Home*, and you start with the Goal of organizing the closets. You could slowly sort through all the items in the closet and carefully examine and analyze each one like it's a rare gem you're about to purchase, or you could race through the process, chucking anything questionable into a garbage bag. When we wanted to turn our garage into a game room, we discovered the contractors were arriving that morning—days ahead of schedule, which they claimed they had told my husband—and our garage was packed from floor to ceiling with boxes, old furniture, and lawn tools. After having procrastinated for months, Eric and I got that garage cleared out in one hour. Many people on Craigslist were very happy that day.

Work Faster

Now your D-I-A Goal, for the Desire *Start a Side Hustle*, is to launch a business selling meal plans. Challenge yourself to get your website up and running in four hours. Yes, it can be done! What is the quickest platform to get up and running? What will you have to *not* do in order to make your deadline?

Travel Faster

Well, don't actually *travel* faster unless you enjoy getting speeding tickets. What I mean is, for the D-I-A Desire *Travel*, don't over-analyze each of the many options for your trip, from accommodations to the rental car to what to pack. That's a sure ticket to overwhelm, not Paris. Instead, quickly make decisions and move on. For example, when we went to Tokyo, I could have spent days researching Airbnb options alone. Entire home or private room? Stay in which of the eight zillion regions of Tokyo? Instead, I looked at the top-reviewed apartments in our price range that were near a large subway station, picked one that looked acceptable, and booked the space. And it ended up being awesome!

Will yourself to pick up the pace when working on your D-I-A Plan (or anything else, for that matter), and you'll get much more done in much less time.

Chapter 30

Talk to Yourself

Several years ago, my writer friend Jennifer and I would hold what we called *Boot Camp Days* every week: We'd call each other on the hour, every hour, and share what we got done in the last hour and what we planned to do in the next one. There were no repercussions if we didn't get done what we said we'd do, but somehow we would both be super-productive on those Boot Camp Days. There was something about telling someone what we planned to do each hour that helped clarify and solidify it in our minds, and also delete the temptation to turn to easy tasks instead of working on our harder-but-more-important projects.

We no longer do Boot Camp Days, but I've discovered the secret of how to achieve the same effect without an accountability buddy: Before you start work on a D-I-A Goal, tell yourself, out loud, what your plan is. Your brain will snap to attention, and you'll get the job done.

I researched this phenomenon to find out if there's any science behind how it works. Turns out there is! For example, this is from an article in *Spirituality & Health* magazine called "The Surprising Benefits of Talking to Yourself": "*The Quarterly Journal of Experimental Psychology* published results of a study in which 20 volunteers were shown lots of pictures of objects, and told to pick the one showing a banana. Half did the task quietly, and the other half repeated the word *banana* out loud the whole time. The self-talkers found the picture of the banana a little faster."

Focus and concentration, check. Easily obtained bananas, check. Now, how about taking care of the overwhelm? One of the nine benefits listed in the article is this one: "Many people with ADD talk to themselves to help bring a tangle of thoughts into focus. Notice how often you see athletes muttering under their breath before an event; they're calming themselves down and pumping themselves up. It works."

When you're about to delve into your D-I-A Plan for the day, chances are your mind is screaming at you that there are 50 other things you could be doing right now, and every single one of them, including polishing the stainless steel in the kitchen, is more important than this one. But if you say out loud to yourself, "Okay, in the next hour I'm going to research foreign language classes at the community center and sign up for the best one," you've settled it. That's what you're going to do, because you told yourself so!

Talking to yourself isn't crazy—it's one more tactic that can help you pursue a full and rich life, so try it today to get into practice before starting your D-I-A Plan. I don't care where you are: Even if you talk to yourself in the middle of the supermarket, people will just think you're an important businesswoman wheeling and dealing into her Bluetooth. Or maybe they *will* think you're crazy. Who cares?

PART 4

The Do-It-All Plan

"It is better to wear out than to rust out." —President Millard Fillmore

Your mind is ready. Your calendar is ready. You're feeling the energy and motivation! Let's get started with the D-I-A Plan that will help you, well, do it all.

In the following chapters you'll get more info on the Plan, plus on each of the D-I-A Desires and how to accomplish them.

Chapter 31

About the D-I-A Plan

I am so psyched, and I hope you are, too! You're finally ready to have a go at your D-I-A Plan. C'mon, stand and pump your fist in the air! I am *totally* doing that right now.

In the D-I-A Plan, you'll be adding one Desire—one new activity, event, experience, skill, or accomplishment—to your life at a time. For each Desire you'll be filling out the corresponding Desire Worksheet, and using the other Worksheets, as instructed in the next chapter, to help keep you motivated and on track. Once you've reached a Desire, you'll then move on to the next one in the same way.

Of course, *doing it all* means different things for different people, but after speaking with women about what kinds of experiences they want to have, and what memories they want to create, I synthesized the results into these 12 Desires:

1. Love Your Looks
2. Travel
3. Create an Amazing Home
4. Cross a Finish Line
5. Entertain
6. Volunteer
7. Write
8. Become Well-Read
9. Start a Side Hustle
10. Gain Mad Skills
11. Grow your Spiritual Practice
12. Do More Stuff with the People You Love

Now, I know these are big, nebulous Desires. Love your looks? Travel? What do these mean, and how do you know when you're done? In the Worksheet for each Desire, you'll be able to brainstorm what each Desire means to you, what it will look like when you're done, and how to make it happen.

If you love the idea of a particular Desire, but aren't sure what it means to you, feel free to choose one of the Goals I suggest; I selected Goals based on availability, accessibility, and the ability to reach them without spending a ton of cash...though you certainly *can* spend a ton of cash on any of these if you'd like to!

For each Desire you'll find three *Levels* of Goals to help you if you're feeling stuck:

Level 1: The easiest goal for most people. Do this and you'll have one more notch in your D-I-A belt, and an easy win that will motivate you to do even more.

Level 2: If you've already accomplished Level 1 and don't want a repeat, or if you feel all fired up from the easy win—or if Level 1 just doesn't float your boat—Level 2 is for you.

Level 3: If you're ready to go after a big challenge, this is true mastery of your D-I-A Desire.

For example, for the D-I-A Desire *Write*, the three Levels of suggested Goals are:

Level 1: Get a guest post published on one of your favorite blogs.

Level 2: Start your own blog on the topic of your choice.

Level 3: Write a book.

I want every reader to get what she truly wants out of this book, so you can select your own Goals for each Desire—or if you're undecided, simply pick one from the three Goals I recommend.

More on the Desires

In Chapter 33, *The Desires*, for each D-I-A Desire you'll find details on exactly what it is and why it's important, and strategies for making that Desire a reality. And since it's key that your D-I-A Desires fulfill your personal values, I offer a chart with examples of how each Desire fulfills four values I randomly chose from the list of values included in the Values Checklist, which you'll find in your free downloadable package of Worksheets. These charts are not meant to tell you what your values should be, or how you should make your Desires fit them; they're meant to spur your brainstorming process and show you how to look at your D-I-A Desires from the perspective of *your own* personal values.

Right now, chances are one or two of these Desires are not exactly rocking your world. Please check out the info I've provided on each Desire, and see if it doesn't convince you. Also, be sure to fill out the Worksheets for each Desire, because even if on the surface a Desire seems like it isn't a match for your lifestyle or values, after filling out the Worksheet you may discover it actually is.

If, after all that, you still feel any of the D-I-A Desires really aren't for you, you can swap them out with a Desire of your choosing. For example, maybe you want to go after Desires in the realm of Health, Romance, Parenting, or Career. I've included a blank Worksheet for just this reason.

Know you don't like a particular Desire, but aren't sure what to replace it with? I have a Worksheet for that, too! There, you'll be brainstorming what you want to create, what's missing in your life, and more.

And if you're looking at a Desire in the Plan and thinking, "Yeah I got that"—for example, you already run marathons and the D-I-A Desire is to participate in an athletic event, or the D-I-A Desire is *Write* and you're already a professional writer—you can always choose a new form of the Desire you haven't tried before. A marathon runner can sign up for a powerlifting competition. A professional sci-fi author can pen a memoir.

I'm not going to make you complete one Desire per month, because it wouldn't make sense, even if it does come out to a nice, round year. Some Goals can be completed in the same month you start them, while others will likely extend into future months. For example, *Create an Amazing Home* may take a few days if your Goal is to paint the living room and buy new throw pillows, or it may take a few months if your Goal involves knocking down walls.

The Order of the Desires

I started out with a Desire that will help you feel incredible, so afterward you can tackle the other D-I-A Desires from a space of total awesomeness. I also alternated easier Desires with harder ones, though this is subjective, depending on what each Desire means to you. I put a lot of thought into the order of the D-I-A Desires, but if it doesn't work for you, feel free to switch them around.

Just don't use this leeway as an excuse to move scarier or harder Desires to the end of—or totally off—the list! The D-I-A Plan is designed to get you to stretch yourself right out of your comfort zone. Otherwise, why bother?

And now…onward!

Chapter 32

How to Use the Worksheets

I'm excited to offer you Worksheets that will help you reach your D-I-A Desires. You can download a package of printable Worksheets for free at:

www.therenegadewriter.com/D-I-AWorksheets

The bonus downloadable package includes not only the 12 D-I-A Worksheets and the Values Checklist, but also many other Worksheets that will let you put into action the strategies from earlier in the book. You'll also find one of each Worksheet in the Appendix at the end of this book.

I'd like to explain what all the Worksheets are and how to use them. I also included the instructions right on each Worksheet, so you don't need to refer back to the book as you fill them out.

Values Checklist

This is a huge list of common personal values (see Chapter 5, *Give Your Values Center Stage*, for more info). Pick the top three values that resonate with you most, or that you most want to live by. You'll want to do this one before beginning the any of the D-I-A Plan Worksheets, as the personal values you choose will have an impact on your answers to the questions on these Worksheets.

After you choose your top three values, you'll head down to the end of the worksheet and brainstorm about what each value means to you.

all, *achievement* or *love* or *stability* can mean something very different to different people. Don't worry about prioritizing your values. Does it really matter if *autonomy* slightly edges out *balance*? Maybe in some of your D-I-A Desires it will, in which case you can worry about that when it happens, and let your gut decide.

This is not a test. If you choose three values and later decide they weren't the right ones, you can always change them. My top values have morphed over time as my life has changed, and as I came to realize that maybe *security* was conflicting with *freedom*, so I should choose *health* or *wealth* instead.

Tolerations List

As we discussed in Chapter 17, *Become More Intolerant*, here's where you'll go through each category of your life, from your health to your appliances, and list 100 things that are bugging the heck out of you. You'll also need your Tolerations List to complete the 12 D-I-A Plan Worksheets.

Killed Tolerations List

Got rid of a toleration? Awesome! Add it here so you can look back on the list occasionally and experience a bump in pride and motivation, as we talked about in Chapter 14, *Go Back for the Future*.

To-Don't List

This is from Chapter 19, *Before To-Do, Try To-Don't*. Before filling out each D-I-A Plan Worksheet, use the To-Don't List to make a list of the obligations and tasks you'll cut out of your life to make more time and mental space for your current D-I-A Goal. You can pull from your Tolerations List for this, too.

Night-Time Brain Dump List

This is an all-purpose list you can use to clear your head before bed, as mentioned in Chapter 23, *Sleep Less*. Use this Worksheet nightly to list everything that's on your mind so these to-dos and unresolved issues don't keep you awake all night. The next day, you can go through the list with a fresh perspective and take care of, schedule, delete, or delegate the items on it.

Rule of Four List

In Chapter 28, we talked about the Rule of Four. Use this Worksheet whenever you're feeling overwhelmed and want to pare down your to-do list to your top priorities.

Admin Day To-Do List

Remember the Admin Day we discussed in Chapter 26? Use this Worksheet every week as a handy place to jot down any necessary tasks that aren't in service of your D-I-A Desires, and that can wait a few days without the Earth imploding, so you can get to them on your Admin Day.

Did List

We talked about this in Chapter 14, *Go Back for the Future*. Here's where you'll list everything you accomplished in the past day or week, so you can look back on your accomplishments and be treated to a healthy dose of energy and motivation.

Naikan Worksheet

This one is from Chapter 16, *Practice Extreme Gratitude*. Skyrocket your gratitude—and your joy, energy, and motivation—by answering these three questions daily.

1. What did I receive from others today?
2. What have I given to others today?
3. What troubles and difficulties did I cause others today?

The Blank Desire Worksheet

If you want to replace a D-I-A Desire with one of your own, use this blank Worksheet.

The Missing Desire Worksheet

If you've determined that you dislike one of the D-I-A Desires in the Plan, but aren't sure what Desire to replace it with, this Worksheet will help you figure out what you'd like to accomplish next. You can fill this one out when you're ready to get started on that Desire.

The Recap Worksheet

Save this for after you complete the D-I-A Plan. In this Worksheet, you'll free-write about your D-I-A experience using the prompts I provide, to figure out where you want to go from there.

The 12 D-I-A Plan Worksheets

This is the big one: The actual Worksheets where you'll be brainstorming, planning, and achieving your D-I-A Desires. Here, I'll go over each question, so you know why it's there and how to answer it:

What does this Desire look like to me?

Here, you'll choose Goals that resonate with you and make you feel joyful, motivated and excited. If you can't think of one, again, feel free to select one of the three suggested Goals I provide just for that reason.

How does this D-I-A Desire fit at least one of the top three Personal Values I circled on the Values Checklist?

This is where the Values Checklist comes in. As we discussed in Chapter 5, *Give Your Values Center Stage*, your D-I-A Desires need to resonate with your values, or you won't want to bother with all the work it takes to accomplish them. To help you if you get stuck, in the descriptions of each D-I-A Desire in Chapter 33, I offer a chart with examples of how you can make each Desire fit various core values. I randomly chose these values from the Values Checklist, so you'll get an idea of how even the most seemingly incompatible Value-Goal pairs can work. *Write* with *Leadership*? *Love Your Looks* with *Spirituality*? Yes!

Here's an exercise to help me get unstuck: What if I went after the most outrageous manifestation of this Desire? What would it look like?

If all your ideas for going after your D-I-A Goals feel flabby and ineffective, one way to get unstuck is to imagine what you would do if you had to make your Desire a thousand times bigger. For example, if you're working the D-I-A Desire *Start a Side Hustle*, maybe your Goal is to earn a little pocket cash selling your crocheted wine bottle gift bags online. But what if you were instead to build a wine-bottle-gift-bag enterprise with 2,000 employees and a giant HQ in California, and to have your crocheted gift bags featured in top magazines, flaunted by celebrities, and sold by the millions?

Don't be timid. Go *big* with your imagined Goals! After all, they're only in your head—for now, anyway.

Now, what would I do to make these outrageous Goals happen?

Here's where it gets real: If you were to build this gigantic crocheted gift bag corporation, what would you do to make it happen? How would you get millions of your products into people's hands? What would you have to do to be in a position to hire 2,000 employees? How would you get your product featured in the media? Write down your ideas here, and don't be afraid to get a little crazy.

How can I apply any of these crazy ideas and tactics to my actual D-I-A Goals?

I'm not expecting you to actually launch a company that produces millions of crocheted gift bags every year, though you certainly can if you want. But the exercise above probably shook loose whatever was keeping you stuck, and you came up with some fabulous ideas. Can you scale down any of these ideas to realize your actual Goals?

What if I had to achieve my D-I-A Goals in one month or I would literally die? What would I do to make it happen?

This trick is a great excuse-buster from my book *Commit: How to Blast Through Problems & Reach Your Goals Through Massive Action.* You may be racking your brain for ideas on how to accomplish a D-I-A Goal, and complaining that you don't have the time to train for a martial arts tournament, organize your kitchen cabinets, or write a play. But if your doctor said you'd better do it or you'll die, you would sure as heck *find* the time.

Here's where I'll break it down: What steps do I need to take to get my D-I-A Goal rolling?

Once you've decided what tactics you'll be using in order to reach your D-I-A Goal, chunk these down into small bites. For example, for *Love Your Looks*, you may have chosen my suggested Level 3 Goal of overhauling your wardrobe. You might break it down like this:

- Look through recent issues of *Vogue* and *More* magazines to see what the latest fashion trends are.
- Examine all the clothes in my closet. What do I love? What goes together? What needs to be tossed? What will look better if I add a new scarf, belt, or piece of jewelry? What needs to be repaired or refitted?
- Ask my best friend to come over and give me an honest assessment of the clothing I have now.
- Make a list of items I need in order to complete my new wardrobe.
- Research online to see which stores carry the items I need. Are there any local consignment shops or second-hand stores that may have some of these pieces for less?
- Head out to the stores.
- Look up local tailors, and choose the one with the best reviews.
- Bring clothes that need to be repaired or refitted to the tailor.

Now a big, nebulous Goal is turned into a concrete, doable list of actions.

Here's exactly where and when I'll take those steps:

Studies show that people who decide ahead of time exactly when and where they'll complete a task have a much higher rate of compliance, and you can use this question to make sure you follow the steps of your D-I-A Goals. It's a lot like the old game Clue: "Colonel Mustard killed Mrs. White in the drawing room with a lead pipe." Your answers might look like this for various Goals:

- "I'll ask Allie to give me wardrobe tips when I see her this Tuesday at the book club."
- "I'll call my friend in LA on my way home from work on September 19, and see if we can come for a visit."
- "I'll paint the bedroom on Saturday, March 4, starting at 8 am."
- "I'll sign up for a blogging platform and choose a free theme for my new blog at 9 pm on August 25."

See how that works better than just saying, "I'll get my blog started one of these days"?

Let me schedule these tasks into my calendar right now. ___ I'm done!

As we discussed in Chapter 24, *Have an Agenda*, scheduling your to-dos in your calendar keeps less-important tasks from encroaching into your D-I-A Plan time.

Let me look into the future and imagine I'm about to do X. If I foresee any obstacles, what can I do right now to make those future obstacles non-issues?

Ryan Holiday explains in his book *The Obstacle Is the Way*, "We look to envision what could go wrong, what will go wrong, in advance, before we start. Far too many ambitious undertakings fail for preventable reasons. Far too many people don't have a backup plan because they refuse to consider something might not go exactly as they wish."

That's what this question is all about. Say your Goal is to start a blog. Your answers here might be:

- "My kids sometimes aren't asleep by 9 pm, so I'll ask my spouse to put them to bed on Mondays and Wednesdays."
- "The spare bedroom is the only quiet space in the house, but isn't set up for work, so I'll buy a small desk on Craigslist and set it up in the corner."
- "Sometimes I get sucked into a TV show at nine because I want to relax, so I'll record my favorite shows and relax with a cup of chamomile tea while I work on the blog."

Now, when 9 pm rolls around, you'll be ready no matter what obstacles life throws at you.

Can I enlist help with my Goal? (For example, can I ask a friend or family member, join an online community devoted to this Goal, find a mentor, or hire a pro?) Yes___ No___

In Chapter 18, *Get Support*, I got on my soapbox about the importance of getting help when you need it. So that's what this question is for!

If so, what kind of help can I enlist?

Here, you can brainstorm people, services, apps, communities, and so on that can help you reach your D-I-A Goal. The trick to brainstorming is to *not* edit yourself, *not* judge your ideas, and just blast out as many options as you can. This will help shake the chaff from your brain, so you can then go through the list and find the wheat.

Write down the names of friends who may help you, pros you can hire, services you can use, apps and online communities you find…and don't give a thought yet to how you can convince your friend or afford the pro. That's for the next question.

Brainstorm time! Here's who I'll be asking for help, where to find them, how I'll approach them, and how (if they're hired pros or paid services) I can pay for them.

Here's where you worry about how you'll get the help you want. For example, if money is tight, you could:

- Ask for a discount for paying in full up front.
- Ask for a payment plan.
- Join a free online community.
- Ask a skilled friend to help you.
- Barter.
- Join a free local group, such as a running group.
- Ask for a scholarship (for example, for an online class).
- Cut out the cable subscription and use the savings toward hiring help.

Brainstorm how you'll get your hands on the help you want, no matter what it takes. Remember, doing it all is not normal, so don't worry about being normal in your ideas and your approach!

If someone is watching me on a screen as I work on this D-I-A Goal, how would this person know I'm actually working hard?

In Chapter 7, *Do Actual Work*, we talked about the concept of imagining that someone is watching you on a screen, and your objective is to show that person how hard you're working. So if your D-I-A Goal is to volunteer at the soup kitchen, the creepy voyeur will see you at the soup kitchen cooking or ladling out food. If your D-I-A Goal is to read ten classic novels, the Peeping Tom would see you sitting in a chair, flipping pages as you read *Great Expectations*. Write down your ideas for concrete action here.

How can I automate this D-I-A Goal, or parts of the Goal?

In Chapter 27, *Put It on Auto*, you learned several tactics for automating tasks, and you can probably come up with more on your own, too, depending on your exact Goals. If you're stuck, Google *How to automate household tasks*, *How to automate office work*, or whatever fits your current D-I-A Goal for some great ideas you may not have thought of.

If I feel overwhelmed while working on this D-I-A Goal, I'll try these practices to banish the overwhelm and get back to work. (Naikan, meditation, exercise, yoga, a hot bath, etc.)

In Part 2, *The Attitude Adjustment*, I offered lots of strategies for putting the kibosh on fear, excuses, and overwhelm. Which of these resonate with you right now, as you're about to embark on this D-I-A Goal?

Here are the top ten tolerations I'll be getting rid of while I work on this D-I-A Goal, and how I'll do it:

Pull 10 tolerations from the 100 annoyances you listed on your Tolerations List, and use this space to brainstorm ideas on how to banish them. This will give you small wins that will keep your motivation up throughout this Goal, not to mention that it will open up space in your mind and in your life for your new Goal to happen.

Further thoughts/inspirations/brainstorms: Anything else you want to write goes here! Maybe you want to hash out exactly how to approach your best friend for help starting your side hustle, or work out some ideas for automating a certain task. I can't account for every possible situation in the Worksheets, so this is your chance to make the Plan fully your own.

Now...on to the D-I-A Desires!

Chapter 33

The Desires

Now, we're ready to talk about the 12 Desires I've included in the D-I-A Plan. Again, keep in mind that you can always replace a Desire that doesn't resonate with you with one that does. But if you want to follow the Plan as-is, here's a complete description of each Desire.

Desire #1: *Love Your Looks*

You look into the mirror every day and can't help but say, "Hello, Foxy!" You feel attractive, confident, and hot-hot-hot! That's what I want for you now, so it sets you up for feeling fabulous as you blast through the rest of your D-I-A Plan.

Why this Desire?

They say it's what's inside that counts. But that doesn't obviate the fact that when you look good, you *feel* good, and that translates into increased energy, a higher happiness quotient, and treating others better. That's why I included *Love Your Looks* as part of the D-I-A Plan. How wonderful it can feel to be productive, create memories, make things happen, develop a full life—and love how you look while doing it!

The value match:

If your top value is:	Here's how you can make a match.
Spirituality	Think about how important it is for you to honor your creator or the universe by taking great care of your body, inside and out.
Creativity	You can be creative not only with art, writing, and music, but also with your personal style.
Humor	You can show humor and wit through your clothing, jewelry and makeup choices.
Wealth	People who look good tend to land better jobs and earn more.

What do you mean by *Love Your Looks?*

We're busy women. Who has the spare hours to carefully coif their hair, slather on youth-enhancing lotions and potions, and put on a full face of makeup every day? And maintaining a mani/pedi? Forget it. Also, if looking great requires us to lose weight or go under the knife (or needle)—way to bring on the body image issues!

Don't freak: There is no gold standard for looking great, and you get to define what that is for you. What we're *not* talking here about is striving to meet some external standard, such as trying to look like the airbrushed models in the *Sports Illustrated* swimsuit issue, or growing your hair long because supposedly dudes like it better that way. After all, the dudes aren't the ones who have to deal with it every day. No one is expecting you to go on a crash diet or open a line of credit with a plastic surgeon!

This D-I-A Desire does not require you to morph into a size two blonde with an impressive bosom—though if you already are one, great! I don't want to disparage women of *any* size or shape. What we're talking about here is loving the way you look. You want to look at yourself in the mirror and be happy with what you see every day. The purpose of this Desire is for *you* to decide what would make you feel like a million bucks.

One of my favorite quotes, from cosmetics magnate Helena Rubinstein, captures this concept perfectly: "There are no ugly women, only lazy ones." What this means is that even if you're not what society deems conventionally beautiful at this moment (which applies to 99% of the population), you can still be beautiful by taking great care of yourself.

The bare basics of looking fabulous are healthy skin and nails, a hairstyle that flatters your face, and clothes that fit well, compliment your shape, and are in good repair. From this base you can go as far as you want—from a weekly manicure to quarterly visits with a personal stylist.

Stuck? Here are some suggested Goals:

Level 1: Update your hairstyle.
Level 2: Improve your skincare routine and update your makeup.
Level 3: Revamp your wardrobe.

How do I make it happen?

Having written for many of the women's magazines, including beauty features where I interviewed cosmeticians, dermatologists, celebrity hairstylists and more, I gleaned some helpful techniques for accomplishing whatever Goal you choose for this Desire. Take what you like and leave the rest. In the worksheet for this D-I-A Desire, you'll have a chance to jot down some ideas of your own.

Do it yourself. You'll find loads of free YouTube tutorials on applying makeup, adding highlights or lowlights to your hair, and more. If you want you can drop some cash at the salon, but home hair color products have come a *long* way in the last few years. Fashion magazines and their websites offer instructions on everything from how to cut your own bangs to how to achieve the smoky eye look.

Ask your buddies. You probably have a friend, relative, or co-worker who always looks smashing. Ask her if she'll give you makeup tips, critique your wardrobe, or suggest a good hairstylist who works with your hair type.

Bring in the pros. Not sure what makeup colors flatter your skin tone? Make an appointment with a specialist at a department store cosmetics counter. It's free, but you can buy a small item as payment. Want a new hairstyle or color, but you're not sure whether to go with a brunette bob or a pink pixie cut? Book a consultation with the best hair pro in your area. Clueless about clothes? Hire a personal shopper or stylist for one session, then use what you learn to put outfits together on your own in the future.

When I decided to become a personal trainer, I wanted to give my wardrobe an upgrade. I hate shopping, and my closet literally had two wearable tops in it, both of which were black T-shirts. The shopper grilled me about my lifestyle and color preferences, spent a day shopping, and then held a private try-on session where I decided which items to buy. The final price tag was weighty, but that included a brand-new wardrobe full of great-looking pieces, some of which I still wear several years later, and an education on the styles, colors, and shapes that look good on me.

Make skincare a habit. A simple skincare routine can make your skin glow. For example, every time you shower, get into the habit of exfoliating, shaving your legs, using a foot file, applying lotion, and swiping on some nail oil. Every evening, remove your makeup, apply night cream, and repeat the lotion-and-nail-oil routine on your hands. This is just an example; feel free to devise a routine that works for you.

Tiny habits like these will add ten minutes to your daily routine, but will make a big impact on how you look and feel every day. I remember how in Tim Gunn's book *A Guide to Quality, Taste & Style*, he huffed something along the lines of, "Ladies, *please* put on lotion after your shower!" So I guess I'm not the only one who tends to cut corners and suffer the beauty consequences.

Get your clothes tailored. Why roll up your jeans cuffs, tug at blouses that sag at the shoulders, and wear jackets that bunch up around the middle, when a trip to the tailor can make your clothes fit perfectly and flatter your figure?

It's pretty rare that clothing will fit right off the rack. For example, it seems almost every pair of jeans was designed for someone who's six feet tall. I've started bringing my denim to a local tailor and getting it hemmed to the length that works with the shoes I plan to wear with it. According to StyleCaster, getting jeans hemmed should cost around $10, so you can buy an inexpensive pair and end up with perfectly fitting jeans for a quarter of the price of designer denim. If you enjoy sewing, skip the tailor and do the alterations yourself to save even more.

Repair your shoes. Shoes can make or break an outfit, so make sure yours are clean and in good repair. Also, if you invest in high-quality shoes, you can save cash in the long run by keeping them maintained so you can wear them for years. Shoe repair shops can replace run-down heels, repair tears in seams, bring back shine, and more. Every fall, I take my favorite few pairs of boots to the repair shop to bring them back to like-new condition.

Mix high and low. My experience with the personal shopper taught me that wearing all cheap clothing makes a woman look frumpy and messy, but sporting only pricy or flashy items looks desperate—and is expensive. Try pairing a $10 T-shirt from Target with a designer skirt that fits you like a glove, a pricy cashmere cardigan with a bargain-basement scarf, and your blingiest top with your most minimal trousers.

You can mix high and low with makeup, jewelry, skincare products, and haircare products, too, so you'll drop your bucks only where they have the most impact. Use a pricy night cream on your face, and then slather Vaseline on your hands and nails. Get eyeshadow from the one-dollar rack and splurge on fancy foundation. I use a $40 leave-in conditioner and $4 hairspray.

Opt for light over heavy. When it comes to makeup, fragrance, and hair products, a light touch is usually best, unless lots of bright makeup is your signature style and makes you feel fabulous—in which case, go for it! But in general, you don't want astronauts to be able to see your eyeliner from space, and your fragrance shouldn't precede you into a room.

Get out of your rut. Let's take a hint from the late, great David Bowie and make some *ch-ch-ch-changes*. If you've been wearing the same hairstyle since the 80s, have to have your makeup custom blended because the cosmetics companies no longer make your fave colors, or are a VIP customer at a clothing store because it's the only place you shop, then maybe it's time to shake things up. You wouldn't believe how much cosmetics, hair cutting techniques, lotions, self-tanners, hair dye, clothing construction, and more have improved over the last several years!

I learned this lesson through experience. I used to buy all my clothes from the same shop, from jeans to dresses to tops. I was at a restaurant one day, wearing a sundress and black sandals from this store, and saw another woman wearing the exact same outfit! I decided it was high time to expand my personal style. So the next time I went shopping, instead of running into and out of my favorite shop and calling it a day, I checked out every women's clothing store in the area, and ended up finding gems at the most unexpected places—like a shop that is clearly meant for Bohemian-type teens, and a higher-end store I'd never even heard of. Mixing and matching pieces from different shops, along with the clothing I already owned, let me create a wardrobe that was less matchy-matchy and more *me*.

These techniques should give you some direction on this D-I-A Desire. Now, head on over to the Worksheet for this Desire, where you can brainstorm how to make it happen for *you*.

Desire #2: *Travel*

If there's one thing people remember, it's a trip. You may not recall the ending of that hot Netflix series you binge-watched last year, but you will definitely remember a trip to Europe, Mexico, New York City, Africa, or even somewhere close to your home.

Why this Desire?

Traveling benefits many areas of your life, and plays well with many of the other Desires in the D-I-A Plan as well. For example:

- Travel can help you relax. I'm not necessarily talking about a jaunt to some tropical isle—any trip that gets you away from your daily chores and to-do list can be relaxing, even if it's just a short drive away from where you live.
- Travel is an educational experience for you and your family.
- If you read up on the destination, learn what's happening there, and even read some of the literature from that region, travel can help you become more well-informed and well-read.
- Volunteer vacations can count toward the D-I-A Desire *Volunteer*.
- Traveling offers you a new perspective, which may make you want to change the way you do things at home.
- Traveling helps you bond with your loved ones. My son and I love to laugh about how shocked we were in Tokyo to find out a certain restaurant dish was not rice with poppy seeds as we'd thought, but hundreds of teeny tiny whole fish.

The value match:

If your top value is:	**Here's how you can make a match.**
Community	Explore your own region through travel, getting to know the towns near you and the people who live there. Go on day trips to volunteer, or to participate in charity events.
Self-reliance	Travel solo!
Success	For career or financial success, connect your adventures to book tours, client visits, or industry trade shows.
Peace	Plan trips to locations you find relaxing, such as the beach or the mountains, or try a retreat or wellness spa vacation.

What do you mean by *Travel*?

It's really up to you, and depends on your schedule, your lifestyle, and what you consider fun. Your Goal might be a day trip to a nearby town that boasts historical reenactments, or a year-long sailing vacation. You decide!

Stuck? Here are some suggested Goals:

Level 1: Go on two day trips in one month.
Level 2: Take a trip of at least two nights to a location outside your state or region.
Level 3: Go on an overseas trip.

How do I make it happen?

You don't need to be independently wealthy to travel, and the more you do it, the easier it will be. For example, we're a middle-class family with two working parents, a young kid, and usually an exchange student (who we take on domestic trips), and we travel several times per year. Here are some of the tactics we've gleaned through experience:

Mix work and play. If you or your partner travel for business, then turn business trips into family trips. For example, my husband represents his employer at board game events all over the world, and his airline tickets are paid for by the company. Often, he'll extend the trip by a few days and our son and I will come along, meaning we need to buy only two tickets instead of three. On our trip to Tokyo in 2015, Eric's employer also agreed to compensate us for part of our lodging if our son and I helped Eric out at a one-day board game convention.

Hack your travel. Many wanderers use special tactics to save loads on travel, like strategically using credit cards and airline loyalty programs to rack up airline miles and hotel points, and score free vacations. I'm not sure if this qualifies as a hack, but last year I received an $800 voucher from Delta and a first-class ticket on the next flight out by giving up my seat on a crowded plane. Later, I used part of that voucher for a free trip to Boston. Look up *travel hacks* online for tons of tips, and I like the MillionMileSecrets.com blog, which offers advice specifically geared for beginners.

Forget hotels. Accommodations can put a big dent in your wallet. Luckily, services have sprung up that can help you save wherever you stay. For example, on Airbnb.com people rent out rooms in their homes, and even whole apartments and houses, at a fraction of the price of a hotel or vacation rental. When we went to Tokyo last year, hotels cost $200 and up per night, but we scored a one-room apartment via Airbnb for just $70 per night. On Couchsurfing.com, people open their homes to travelers for free. And don't forget staying with friends, which we do on most of our trips!

Bring your own food. Eating on the road is a big expense. Not only are there three squares per day, but someone inevitably gets hungry between meals and you have to shell out for a snack at some overpriced store or restaurant. I always pack portable treats that don't need refrigeration, like granola bars, apples, and Babybel cheese rounds, so we don't need to spend any cash when hunger pangs hit between meals. If you're going on a day trip in your car, you can even bring full meals and bottles of water in a cooler.

Remember where you live. Do you live close to a big city, but have never been to the hotspots? Maybe you live near San Francisco, but sniff at the idea of visiting Alcatraz because it's so touristy. Or you're close to New York City, but have never checked out the Empire State Building, Statue of Liberty, or September 11 Memorial. Suck it up and go, and you'll find these tourist spots make for fun, cheap trips.

Plan way ahead. Travel planning can become overwhelming fast, so it's essential to start early. For example, as soon as we get an inkling that we might want to go on a trip, we fill out the permission forms for our exchange student's coordinator and school, and contact our son's school and dance studio to ensure the trip won't get in the way of important events like dance rehearsals and recitals.

You can also start a trip to-do list, packing list, and other checklists way ahead of time, so you don't need to worry about those when you're in the thick of things. For example, years ago I created a pre-travel checklist template that I can revise and print out for each trip, so we're sure not to forget some important step like turning down the thermostat, setting the home alarm, or taking out the trash.

Force your hand. Act first, freak out later. Of course my husband and I were nervous about spending money on all those trips in 2015, and about the hassle of planning big trips, so we forced our hand: We bought our plane tickets months in advance, before we had a chance to talk ourselves out of it, and then we *had* to make it work. This strategy works for a lot of other goals as well.

Bring the basics. Worrying over what to pack? After all, you don't want to be a thousand miles from home and realize you forgot to bring your favorite shampoo or book or bracelet! Forget all that. We've learned over the years not to stress over what to bring: If you have your passport, money and credit cards, and medications, you're all set. If you forget anything else and simply cannot go on without it, you can buy it when you get to your destination. One year my husband forgot to pack a coat and underwear on a business trip to Germany, so as soon as he landed, he found a mall and stocked up on what he needed.

So as you can see, our extensive travel in 2015 wasn't a case of a family of wealthy jet-setters hopping onto a plane and flying off into the sunset. Like most people, we needed to be careful with our money, work around school schedules, and do research and prep-work. Was it all worth it? *Hell yes*!

Head on over to the Travel Desire Worksheet so you can start planning some trips of your own.

Desire #3: *Create an Amazing Home*

Now, you're going to work on creating a healthy, beautiful home environment you love to be in, and that will let you and your family have fun, connect, and thrive physically and emotionally.

Why this Desire?

Creating and maintaining a clean, orderly, pleasant, and comfortable home may not seem much like *doing* anything, but for many women I spoke with, this Desire is key to feeling joyful, peaceful, and accomplished. Also, it's hard to feel like a D-I-A warrior when your home is uncomfortable, not decorated the way you like, or just plain messy.

In addition, this Desire ties directly into other D-I-A Desires:

- *Entertain*: You'll need the proper space and supplies, and when people come over, you'll probably want your home looking neat and attractive so everyone can fully relax and enjoy.
- *Write* and *Start a Side Hustle*: It's important that you have a calm, organized space that inspires creativity and focus.
- *Gain Mad Skills*: This D-I-A Desire requires that your home be stocked with what you need. For example, if you want to learn to knit, it's nice to have a space to pursue this hobby, with places to store your needles, yarn, and patterns.
- *Grow Your Spiritual Practice*: It's much easier to pray, meditate, or journal in a calm, peaceful, beautiful space.

The D-I-A Plan is all about creating a meaningful, memorable, and full life, and your home is the place where a lot of your life is lived.

The value match:

If your top value is:	**Here's how you can make a match.**
Friendship	Clean, stock, and decorate one room with your friends in mind. Have plenty of your best friend's favorite wine on hand, purchase a set of cushy chairs to relax in with your buddies, and think about your friends' comfort and health as you clean.
Intimacy	Decorate your living room in a way that creates and grows intimacy, with cozy seating arrangements, warm colors, and candles.

Reputation	Remember that having a beautiful, well-stocked, well-kept home can only do good things for your reputation.
Learning	Make an effort to learn housekeeping, cleaning, and decorating techniques you didn't already know. Also, equip your home with tools that will help you learn: bookshelves full of books, a desk and task lamp for doing your French class homework, educational materials for your kids, and so on.

What do you mean by *Create an Amazing Home*?

The style you choose for your home is your own—I just ask that you honor your style and not continue to live in a home that fails to make you jump up and down with glee whenever you look at or think about it. For example, the first couple years we lived in our current house, we didn't bother to paint the walls. The previous owners had chosen tasteful shades of sage green, light blue, and beige, and it seemed easier to just leave them that way. But over time I felt more and more unsettled because our natural style has always been to revel in bold, vivid colors and patterns. We finally painted our walls rich shades of butternut, lime, teal, and raspberry, and bought new furniture and area rugs to match. When people here in the land of builder beige enter our house they probably think we're nuts—but we don't care. We finally feel at home in our house.

Aside from honoring your personal style, there are a few basics to think about that will work with whatever Goal you choose to pursue for this Desire:

Clean and organized closets and cupboards. Does anyone really feel good when they open a closet door and a six-foot high pile of junk topples over onto them? Or when they go to cook a meal and can't find the colander in the over-stuffed cabinets?

Proper lighting. Misplaced or too-dim lighting makes it hard for you to pursue hobbies and reading, and makes a space look "off." It's amazing how different your home feels when you invest in good lighting. We experienced this when we finally replaced the rickety, dated, and insufficient track lighting in our kitchen with canister lights. I can see, I can see!

Clean, fresh air. I can't overstate the importance of healthy, fresh air in your home—air that's free of cigarette smoke, dust, pollen, bad smells, and other contaminants.

Well-stocked closets, cupboards, and pantry. You want to have fresh sheets and towels always available, the tools to pursue your work and hobbies, a store of your family's favorite foods, and the proper cooking implements and equipment to create healthy, flavorful meals.

Spaces to do what you love. Do you like to meditate? Do you work at home? Maybe your daughter is into video games. If you have space dedicated to the pastimes everyone enjoys, with all the tools they need, you'll feel happier in your home. For example, I set up a corner in our bedroom for meditation and yoga; my husband is heavy into board games, so we converted the garage into a board game room with gaming tables, floor-to-ceiling shelves, and comfortable seating for 12 gamers; and our son loves drawing, so a corner of his room is dedicated to a desk, task lamp, and art kit.

General cleanliness. To promote health, peace, and happiness, your home needs to be as free as possible of dust, dirt, mildew, and mold.

A home isn't just a place where you live: It should fulfill your family's emotional needs, keep you healthy, and make you feel restored and renewed. It should be a refuge from the craziness and demands of the outside world. I hope we can stop regarding housekeeping as demeaning; it's meaningful, important work that can add to your life experience in a positive way.

Stuck? Here are some suggested Goals:

Level 1: Create and implement a one-month plan for cleaning and organizing your home, and keeping it that way.

Level 2: Revamp one room in your home by changing up the wall color and accessories like pillows, artwork, and throw rugs.

Level 3: Make over at least one entire room to be just the way you want it, from paint and flooring to furnishings and equip ment. This may require remodeling!

How do I make it happen?

"Oh, great," you're saying, "instead of doing it all, I'm actually going to be spending 90% of my time polishing the doorknobs and vacuuming the drapes—that is, when I'm not shopping for the perfect throw pillows and changing the HVAC filters."

Not so! In the D-I-A Worksheet for this Desire you'll be able to brainstorm what this Desire means to *you*, and ways you can fit it into your life. But here are a few ideas to get you started.

Go on a cleaning and organizing binge. Blast through an entire room in one day, and you'll feel motivated and refreshed when you gaze upon your newly sparkling space. Invite a friend over to clean and organize one room in your home at a time: Empty the closets and cupboards; sell or donate what you don't need; organize what's left; and scrub down the whole room, from the ceiling to the floor. Then, you can do the same at their house.

Surf the web. I've found tons of great ideas for decorating, cleaning, and organizing on blogs and online magazines. You can also shop online to find unusual, useful household products you won't find at your local department store, like gift-wrap organizing systems, Lego storage units, and library ladders that let you store your books, games, hobby materials, or wine on shelving up to the ceiling.

Get pro design. I have a friend who's an interior designer, so when I need help with a decorating or design decision, I hire her for an hour or two. You don't need to commit to a full package if you want help with just one thing! I'll send my friend photos of our space, and she'll email me back with links to the perfect products, a furniture layout, or a plan I can show to our contractor. It's well worth the $100-$200 to have an expert designer research, plan, and shop so I don't have to. And she does a better job at it, too!

Want to save cash? Home improvement stores like Lowes and Home Depot will help you with your remodeling and flooring projects *gratis*; for example, if you're redoing your kitchen, the experts at these stores will work up a blueprint of which cabinets fit where. Or, head online to use interactive virtual planners (the Home Depot website has one for the kitchen) that let you tinker with potential designs on your own.

Use what you love. My designer friend once told me that if you love it, it will match. When you feel yourself drawn to a painting, candleholder, or piece of furniture, it's probably because it sings to your personal style. If you make all your design choices this way, everything will look great together.

Neaten daily. Before you hit the sack, spend 15 minutes neatening the house: Take out the trash and recycling, fill and run the dishwasher, pick up clothes and books that are lying around, and wipe up any obvious dirt. That way you'll wake up to a home that's fresh and clean, and not come into the kitchen bleary-eyed and needing coffee, only to be met with the mood-killing sight of a stack of food-encrusted dishes. You can also do a quick clean before heading to work so you'll return home to a calm, pleasant environment.

Shop in your community. Community classifieds sites like Craigslist are bursting with household items for sale cheap, from lamps to sofas, not to mention ads from people who are willing to haul away trash, paint, do drywall work, and complete other home-related tasks at an affordable rate. Just make sure the person you hire is qualified and insured! Freecycle boasts over nine million members worldwide. Members post items they want to get rid of for no charge, and can also post items they want. You may find a gem!

Hire help. If you and your family simply hate cleaning, you aren't good at it (and don't care to learn), or you want to make time for other parts of your D-I-A Plan, consider hiring a cleaning service. You can find services at different price points, and you can also hire cleaners for any time interval you want, from once a week to once a month to as-needed. Another option to think about is hiring a professional organizer to take your closets, home office, or cupboards from *argh!* to *ahhh*.

Plan a spring and fall cleaning. Nothing feels better than the sense of renewal you experience when your home is sparkling from top to bottom—when the drapes are laundered, the baseboards are scrubbed, the upholstery is steam-cleaned, the light bulbs are dusted, the walls are washed, and the cabinet interiors are spick and span. You can do this yourself, recruit your family, or hire a local teen or a cleaning service.

Freshen the air. Change your home's HVAC filters regularly, and use air purifiers, humidifiers, or dehumidifiers as needed. Always use the bathroom fan when taking a shower to prevent mold and mildew problems. And unless you live in an area with heavy car traffic, open the windows as much as you can. I've been known to open the windows in the dead of winter to bring in fresh air!

Have extra. Make sure you have more than enough of everything you use in your home; this fosters a feeling of abundance, peace, and gratitude. For example, instead of having one set of sheets for each bed that you wash and re-use every week, keep three sets for each bed: one for now, one for the wash, and one just in case. Buy enough kitchen towels that you can grab a new one as soon as the old one becomes soiled. When your favorite shampoo or paper towels go on sale, buy a dozen. Stock your freezer and pantry with loads of the non-perishable foods your family enjoys.

Keep lists. You can download all kinds of household lists and checklists online, or create them yourself. You may want to keep lists of household to-dos and repairs, items to buy, pantry inventory, weekly meal plans, and more. Many people keep their lists in a household management binder.

Don't get sucked in. You can't buy a nurturing, orderly home. The home furnishings industry would love to sell you a gadget for every imagined need, telling you that this is the one that will make you feel wonderful in your home. But when it comes to creating a home you love to be in, no yogurt maker or set of decorative spice canisters can stand in for the basics of good housekeeping.

On to the Desire #3 Worksheet! There, you'll be able to figure out how this D-I-A Desire fits with your personal values, think about what it means to you, brainstorm ways to realize your chosen Goal, and more.

Desire #4: *Cross a Finish Line*

Imagine yourself sprinting over a finish line, kickboxing an opponent in a ring, or kicking a soccer ball through a goal while onlookers cheer you on. In this portion of the D-I-A Plan, you'll be pinpointing an athletic event to take part in, planning and implementing your training, and participating in the event.

Why this Desire?

The D-I-A Plan is all about having fun, living your best life, being active, and creating memories. Even if you don't win your athletic event, pushing yourself to the max, putting yourself out there, gaining a new skill, and reaching a challenging goal fits all of these D-I-A requirements. Heck, even if you're the last one over the finish line, the feeling of accomplishment you'll experience is amazing. If you've never participated in a sport before, this will really stretch your horizons, and if you're already an athlete, you can try something different for your D-I-A Goal.

The value match:

If your top value is:	**Here's how you can make a match.**
Family	Participate in an event you can do as a family. For example, you'll see many families competing together in 5k races.
Learning	Read books and blogs about how to get started, and how to improve, in your chosen sport.
Balance	Exercise of any kind is a great way to achieve a sense of balance. And if you have a sedentary job or tend to be a couch spud, training for an athletic event moves you closer to a balanced ratio of rest:activity.
Service	Choose an event that donates the proceeds to charity.

What do you mean by *Cross a Finish Line*?

As usual, this is entirely up to you. Luckily, there's no shortage of athletic events and competitions for people of all abilities, interests, and ages. Here are just a few of the many options:

- Thumb wrestling competition (yes, there is a World Thumb Wrestling Championship!).
- Bowling tournament.
- Fitness competition.
- Triathlons: Sprint, Olympic, Half-Iron, and Ironman distances.
- Quidditch match.
- Chessboxing tournament.
- Alpine skiing race.
- Fun runs: Mud runs, color runs, glow runs, chocolate runs, and many more.
- Dressage.
- Bocce ball tournament.
- Fencing.
- Disc golf tournament.

Don't want to go it alone? Consider team sports like:

- Soccer.
- Volleyball.
- Roller derby.
- Dodgeball.
- Badminton.
- Full-contact women's football.
- Kickball.

If you're worried you're too old, too out-of-shape, or too whatever to participate in a sport or athletic event, here's a reality check: You don't need to be an über-fit paragon of health, or a spring chicken, to do something athletic. I've always had major back problems, which finally led to surgery last year, and yet I spent 20 hours a week at the karate dojo when I was in my 30s, participated in a mud run in my

40s, have done 19 years of yoga and 10 of weight training, and had a fabulous time coming in fourth-to-last in a 5k a few years ago. My preschooler got tired, and I had to carry him two-thirds of the way. I saw participants who were elderly, on crutches, and disabled, and they all finished the race.

Stuck? Here are some suggested Goals:

Level 1: Train for and run a 5k.
Level 2: Train for and run a half-marathon.
Level 3: Train for and run a marathon.

How do I make it happen?

So you're ready to sign up and start training for an athletic event or competition. Here's my advice on how to get started:

Pick the right event. The best way to find out what type of event you'll enjoy most is to look online (such as on Active.com) for events in your area, quickly research the types of events that stand out to you, and talk to people who have participated in these events to get the real scoop.

But don't over-analyze. If you're searching and searching for the ultimate perfect event, you'll never get anywhere. As always, action trumps perfection, so stop stalling. Make a list of the contenders, pick one that fits your schedule and budget, and then sign up. If you end up not liking the event after you do it, at least you now have a better frame of reference for picking the next one. And you'll still have the proud memory of having finished the event!

Sign up now, worry later. Just as with travel, I recommend committing to an event *now,* and then figuring out how to make it work. For example, if a half-marathon is your choice, register for a local race that takes place about 12 weeks from now, then haul your butt to figure out what needs to happen next.

Create a plan. Figure out how long it takes to train for your event, and work backward from there. For example, a quick online search shows it can take up to 20 weeks for a beginner to train for a marathon. Then, draft a weekly training plan using resources like the *Runner's*

World magazine website, the REI website, or any one of the many books on marathon training you can borrow or buy.

Decide how serious you want to be. Do you want to participate, or win? Your choice will determine how often and how hard you'll train.

Buddy up. Training with friends is more fun than training alone, and you can also hold one another accountable. Don't have friends who want to train with you? Check out Meetup.com for local groups of athletes who train together, such as a running group. For some events, like 5k runs, you can register a team and come up with a fun team name like "Team of Total Awesomeness" or "The Hot Flashes."

Find an app for that. If you're a do-it-yourselfer, take advantage of the many training and tracking apps available for various sports. For example, the free, popular Couch to 5k app offers an eight-week training plan for beginners.

Work with a trainer. A pro, such as a personal trainer, golf coach, or swimming instructor, can whip you into shape for the event and show you how to improve your game. Or save your dollars by asking an athletic friend to help you out, or by joining a group like Team in Training, where you commit to raising a certain amount for charity in exchange for free training and a trip to the event of your choice.

These are just a few ideas to get you started. In the D-I-A Worksheet for this Desire, you'll be able to do a lot more thinking about what you'd like to do, what resources you'll need, and more.

Desire #5: *Entertain*

Many D-I-A women enjoy a full house: Parties, game nights, movie showings, book clubs, knitting groups, playdates for the kids, you name it. Welcoming friends and relatives into your home is just another part of a full, active life.

Why this Desire?

Time spent with friends and relatives is some of the best time of our lives, so why not pack in as much as we can? Whoop it up before you're too old to whoop!

The value match:

If your top value is:	Here's how you can make a match.
Status	Throw a catered fancy-dress party.
Kindness	If you have friends who are feeling down or lonely, invite them over, along with people you know they would enjoy meeting. If you host a birthday party, ask that guests bring donations to your favorite charity in lieu of a gift.
Optimism	Parties can be so nerve-racking. "What if no one shows?" "What if we run out of food?" They're a great, non-life-threatening way to practice optimism, so when an actual hard time comes, you'll be ready.
Security	You have a solid group of friends and relatives whose company you enjoy, and who enjoy your company. This fosters a safe, secure feeling deep in the squishy parts of your heart.

What do you mean by *Entertain*?

You decide. I'm not going to make you host game nights if you'd rather pierce your eyelids rather than move pawns around a board, and you don't have to host Thanksgiving dinner for 20 if you hate cooking. The options for entertaining are as varied as the people reading this book, from inviting one person over, to packing in as many friends as you can fit. Some examples:

- Cocktail parties.
- Playdates for your kids.
- Ugly sweater parties.
- Movie night.

- Game night.
- Pot-lucks.
- Stitch-and-bitch get-togethers.
- Inviting a friend over for coffee.
- Book clubs.
- Classes (for example, we held our son's homeschool Math Circle at our house).
- Theme parties.
- Asking a few buddies over for pizza.
- Holiday celebrations: Fourth of July, Thanksgiving, National Hot Dog Day (which is July 23, in case you were wondering).
- Barbecues.
- Birthday parties.
- Dinner clubs.
- Wine tastings.
- Family reunions.
- Come-as-you-are parties.
- Murder mystery parties.

I'm sure you can come up with many more ideas that fit your lifestyle, budget, schedule, and tolerance for noise and mess. The idea is simply to have one or more people in your home (or a location you've borrowed or rented) for an enjoyable time.

Stuck? Here are some suggested Goals:

Level 1: Invite at least one person to your home four times in one month.

Level 2: Host a party or event for at least five guests at your home.

Level 3: Plan and pull off a major gathering; this may include an outside location, dozens of guests, catering, and a band.

How do I make it happen?

Reaching your D-I-A Goal can be as simple as committing to invite a friend over for tea and cookies each week, and as involved as hosting a huge family reunion at the Polish Club. Here are strategies that will work no matter what type of entertaining you want to do:

Decide who your peeps are. Who do you want to hang with? This D-I-A Desire is definitely not about inviting people into your home out of a sense of obligation—"I guess we really should invite your brother over for dinner." It's about doing more of what you love. You want to create positive memories, so be sure to have on your A-List only those people whose company you enjoy.

Create a group the easy way. Want to host a book club, dinner club, or other type of group, but don't have enough interested friends? Trust me, two friends do not a book club make. My husband and I have both had great experiences with Meetup.com, where you can start a group that potential members can search for by topic. Running a group costs about $13 per month, and if that's an issue you can charge dues to offset the cost. Meetup groups definitely attract crowds: My husband started a board game group about six months ago, and it now has 150 members! We host about 12 gamers every Tuesday night.

Stock up. If you plan to do frequent entertaining, or institute an open-door policy for friends and relatives to drop by whenever, keep a good stock of snacks you can pull out when needed so you don't have to scramble for goodies to serve. For example, we buy multiple bags of chips and pretzels; always have cheese, crackers, olives, veggies, and hummus around; make sure to have apple juice boxes in the fridge for impromptu playdates; and buy lots of soda, beer, and wine. Other items you may want to have on hand include paper plates, plastic utensils, and extra glasses; you can stock up when they go on sale.

Think about what your guests would like, not only what *you* like; no one in my family drinks beer, wine, soda, or apple juice, but our guests appreciate them.

Get ready. Nothing stinks more than not being able to enjoy your guests because you're in the kitchen frantically putting together snacks or meals, or because you were cleaning or decorating up to the very last second and are now exhausted. Get your home ready as early as you can, and seek out recipes you can make ahead of time and freeze, or at least prepare early in the day. Having a good stock of snacks and drinks on hand is part of this; even if you invite someone over on the spur of the moment, you can rest easy that you'll have something to offer them besides soy sauce packets and water.

Study up. Online you'll find blogs, magazines and websites bursting with tips for making your event easier and more fun. Check out classic books on entertaining, like Martha Stewart's *Entertaining* and Ina Garten's *Barefoot Contessa Parties!*

Know your limits. We all have our limits when it comes to being around other people. While I'd love you to try to stretch those limits a bit for the sake of the D-I-A Plan, don't force yourself to be social when you know it will make you want to do that Sharpie thing with your eyeballs. Know yourself! For example, I'm one of those extroverted introverts: I love being around people...until I don't. Then I need to go lie down in a dark, Sharpieless room. So I try not to stack up too much entertaining all in the same week.

Relax! The purpose of entertaining is to enjoy yourself, and to help your guests relax and enjoy as well. If you're freaking out over the state of the *hors d'oeuvres,* or anxious because one of your guests is late, no one will have a good time. Lighten up, sister!

Ready to start entertaining? The D-I-A Worksheet for this Desire will give you a chance to personalize your Goal, generate ideas, and make a plan to put them into action. Party on!

Desire #6: *Volunteer*

With this Desire, you'll be rolling up your sleeves and reading to at-risk kids, protecting wildlife, restoring monuments, shelving books at the library—whatever volunteer project you feel most passionate about, but have never had the time or energy to tackle before.

Why this Desire?

Many of us look at our lives and wonder how we can contribute more of our awesomeness to make the world a better place. We all have our superpowers, and we want to use them for good! Volunteering is a great way to do that. Many organizations run on volunteer power, and couldn't exist without the efforts of wonderful people like you. Faith-based organizations, the public health industry, social service organizations, museums, and libraries are just a few of the entities that need you.

But volunteering isn't just good for society, it's good for *you*, too. *Psychology Today* reports that volunteers live longer, healthier lives than non-volunteers; develop stronger relationships and are less lonely; earn more money; and have a greater sense of purpose.

The value match:

If your top value is:	**Here's how you can make a match.**
Pleasure	Choose a volunteer opportunity you would truly enjoy. Like animals? Walk dogs at the local shelter. Into music? Offer to play the guitar at the children's hospital.
Adventure	Look for overseas opportunities like researching bottlenose dolphins in Croatia, teaching an after-school program for orphans in Cameroon, or working with pandas in China.
Meaningful work	Volunteering counts as meaningful work in its own right, but if you're talking about your paying job, you can save money you earn from your day job to help a cause you care about. Even if your 9-5 is the pits, and you feel like your position contributes nothing to society, knowing that the income from your work helps others will make it more meaningful to you.
Beauty	Volunteer for an art museum, lend your lawyerly skills to Volunteer Lawyers for the Arts, or offer your services to Look Good Feel Better, which improves the self-esteem and quality of life of people with cancer.

What do you mean by *Volunteer*?

I'll let you say it this time: "It's up to *me*!" Opportunities for volunteering abound. For example, you can try:

Voluntourism. Many companies offer this combo of volunteering and tourism, like Projects-Abroad.org and GlobeAware.org.

Fundraising. Sites like Causes.com and Fundrazr.com let you organize campaigns to raise money for a cause you care about. When my son was 5, he posted a fundraising video to Fundly.com to raise money for the Carolina Tiger Rescue. He raised enough to feed the big cats for one day!

Microvolunteering. Volunteer online in the spare minutes of your day. For example, HelpFromHome.org says you can "Volunteer your time in bite-sized chunks, from your own home, on-demand and on your own terms." Another microvolunteering site is SkillsForChange.com.

Full-time volunteering. The Peace Corps or AmeriCorps are examples of this.

Volunteering within your community. Your church, an animal shelter, the food bank, or a homeless shelter might be able to use your help.

Foreign exchange programs. Yes, this is considered charity work, too! At least the IRS thinks so. You can host foreign students for a few weeks in the summer, a semester, or an entire school year. We've hosted 14 students, and have had a full-year exchange student in our home almost every year since our son was born. So even if you have little ones, this can work for you. As a bonus, we now have lots of people to visit when we travel, killing two D-I-A birds with one stone!

Donation drives. I don't mean giving the junk in your closets to Goodwill, but gathering lots of something and sending it where it's most needed. For example, my husband has run a few Games for Soldiers drives: Individuals and board game companies sent Eric dozens of games, and he boxed them up and mailed them to soldiers in Iraq and Afghanistan who'd expressed a wish for games on AnySoldier.com.

These are only a few broad categories of volunteering. When you dig into it, you'll find many more to fit your passions, schedule, abilities, and budget.

Stuck? Here are some suggested Goals:

Level 1: Volunteer at a local soup kitchen or animal shelter for a month.

Level 2: Commit as a long-term volunteer at the soup kitchen, shelter, library, literacy organization, or non-profit of your choice.

Level 3: Start a volunteer organization for a cause you care about.

How do I make it happen?

You're ready to spread your awesomeness over the world. Here are some techniques for figuring out where to volunteer and how to get started:

Decide on your time. How much time do you have to devote to volunteering? Knowing whether you have one hour per week or one day per week will make a big difference in where you choose to lend a hand.

Consider your skills. Are you a lawyer, artist, writer, builder, gardener, sewing enthusiast, pro cook, publicist, math whiz? You can use any of these skills and more to help out. The math maven can tutor underprivileged kids. The publicist can offer to do free PR work for a non-profit. The sewing pro can sew king-sized pillowcases with drawstrings for foster kids (I found this one on VolunteerMatch). Heck, you don't even need to be a pro: Some friends and I once sewed 80 cat beds for the local cat shelter, and I am *not* a master with the sewing machine.

Turn to the internet. Sites like VolunteerMatch.org let you search for opportunities that fit you exactly: Choose by location, the causes you care about, and the age range the volunteer opportunity is suitable for. GoOverseas.com is one of many sites that list overseas volunteer positions. Also check out your town's official website for opportunities, and ask your online buddies for suggestions.

Use who you know. Do you have an *in* with people or businesses that can donate a needed item, help raise money, or publicize your fundraiser or cause? For example, my husband ran Games for Soldiers drives because he has a lot of contacts in the board game industry.

Recruit your buddies. If you don't want to go it alone, gather a team of volunteers! For example, you could all sign up to help set up at the local farmers market, bag up lunches at the homeless shelter, or knit baby booties for preemies.

Know your heart, and dig deep. Whatever cause you care about, you can find many types of volunteer opportunities beyond the obvious ones. For example, my husband and I are into cat rescue. Sure, we've volunteered at the shelter to feed the cats and change their litter—that's the obvious one. But we also did more off-the-wall types of volunteering that people may not be as aware of: We were volunteer educators, speaking to elementary school classes about the importance of treating animals well; I wrote articles *pro bono* for an ASPCA newsletter; we tapped a friend who's a district manager for a dollar store chain and bought up cases of cat food bowls for the shelter; and we both volunteered at monthly spay/neuter clinics for feral cats, where we did everything from anesthesia, to instrument washing, to cat raking (yes, that's a thing).

So if the normal volunteer opportunities in your chosen cause don't make your heart sing, keep digging, make some calls, and see what else you can do.

In the D-I-A Plan Worksheet for this Desire you'll be reaching into your mind and soul to figure out what is the best volunteer opportunity for you, determining how to get started, and jumping in with both feet—and your heart.

Desire #7: *Write*

Who doesn't have a story, poem, book, blog post, play, or song inside them just waiting to be written down? Maybe my statistics are skewed because I know so many writers, but one of the top things women wish they had is the time, ability, and bravery to write down what's in their souls.

Why this Desire?

Writing is much more than putting words on paper. It's a way to give voice to our fantasies, desires, wishes, and ideas. It helps us creatively work through, and work out, problems and issues, and gives us a way to express who we really are.

An article in the *Independent Collegian* offers up two reasons why creative writing is so important. First, it gives you a better understanding of yourself; second, it gives you a deeper and broader understanding of others.

In addition, whether you share your writing with the world or keep it to yourself, maintaining a writing habit and completing a written work will give you a sense of pride and competence you'll take with you in everything else you do.

If, like me, you are already a long-time or professional writer, choose a Goal that's out of your wheelhouse. For example, a pro blogger can write magazine articles, and a romance author can pen a thriller. My business partner and I are working on a novel—my first one!

The value match:

If your top value is:	Here's how you can make a match.
Authenticity	Developing your voice as a writer and determining what you yearn to write about are great ways to honor your authenticity.
Curiosity	Write on topics you want to know more about; for example, if you've always been interested in the ancient world, how about writing a historical romance set in ancient Greece?
Spirituality	Start a blog based on your religious beliefs or your own personal brand of spirituality.
Leadership	Show the world you know how to write well, and they'll line up to ask you to teach them. Also, you can gain leadership positions through your ability to write persuasively. A well-publicized book or a guest post on an influential blog might convince others to follow your way of thinking.

What do you mean by *Write*?

Dorothy Parker said: "Writing is the art of applying the ass to the seat." I don't care what form of writing you do or what you write about, as long as you develop a consistent writing practice and write toward the goal of completing a work.

Here are some examples of types of writing that may resonate with you. You can write:

- Books.
- Poetry.
- Songs.
- Essays.
- Articles (for newspapers, magazines, or online publications).
- Blog posts (for your own blog, or guest posts for someone else's blog).
- Fan fiction.
- Screenplays.
- Marketing materials for businesses (aka copywriting, which is much more creative than it sounds).
- Editorials.
- Jokes (perhaps for a stand-up comedy routine).

Within each of these types of writing there may be multiple genres to choose from. For example, say you choose the Goal of writing a book. That could mean:

- A novel—like romance, science fiction, fantasy, erotica, mystery, horror, thriller, or Western.
- Fan fiction.
- Nonfiction—like autobiography, memoir, self-help, biography, travelogue, how-to, or creative nonfiction.
- A cookbook.

You may want to sell your writing (like writing guest posts for paying blogs), share your ideas with others for free (such as fan fiction), or keep your writing all to yourself (like an intensely personal memoir).

You don't need to share your writing with the world, but you do need to set a Goal and work your hardest to reach it.

Stuck? Here are some suggested Goals:

Level 1: Get a guest post published at one of your favorite blogs.
Level 2: Start your own blog on the topic of your choice.
Level 3: Write a book.

How do I make it happen?

You asked the right person! Of course, how you start and maintain a writing practice depends on your exact Goal, but I have some advice on how to get started with any form of writing:

Learn the form. Whatever type of writing you want to do, you'll find instructional books, e-books and blogs that will help you learn the ins and outs of that genre. Examples include *Poemcrazy: Freeing Your Life with Words* by Susan G. Wooldridge; *Writing Down Your Soul: How to Activate and Listen to the Extraordinary Voice Within* (on journaling) by Janet Conner; *The Renegade Writer* blog by Diana Burrell and myself, about magazine writing; and *The Screenwriter's Bible* by David Trottier. Heck, even the *Cosmopolitan* website ran an article on how to write fan fiction.

Get a handle on grammar. Some writers say grammar is unimportant and the key thing is to get your ideas across. I disagree. I've bought e-books that are rife with common grammatical errors, and they're so distracting that it's difficult to focus on the point of the writing. If you need help, check out Strunk & White's *The Elements of Style*, which is free online, and Grammar Girl's Quick and Dirty Tips blog.

Stretch yourself. Whatever Goal you choose, make sure it's a type of writing you haven't done much before! If you're already writing two blog posts per week, don't just pick that as your Goal and call it a day; instead, try out a new form.

Challenge yourself. November is National Writing Month, where organizations hold challenges like National Novel Writing Month (otherwise known as NaNoWriMo) and National Nonfiction Writing Month (NaNonFiWriMo), where you have to write a certain amount in 30 days. Joining contests like these, even though you're competing only with yourself, can light a fire under your butt while you connect with like-minded writers. If this Desire falls outside November, you can always round up a group of writers and create a challenge of your own!

Write first, edit later. Write your first draft as quickly as you can, and then go back and edit. Missing information or stuck on a word? Stick in the abbreviation *TK*—editing jargon for *to come*, which comes from the proofreaders' term *tokum*—and keep going; you can fill in the missing details later. If every word needs to be perfect before you'll commit it to paper, your work will never get done. Don't worry about writing crap; first drafts are always crap. Do you know how many times I printed out and edited this entire book—all 200 print pages—by hand? Four times. I also ran the manuscript by my business partner, my writer husband, 20 beta readers, and a professional proofreader.

Learn to love rejection. If you're writing with the goal to be published, you'd better make rejection your friend, because all writers experience it a *lot*—at least if they're trying hard. Some famous examples:

- Ever hear of *The 4-Hour Workweek*, that *New York Times* bestseller that created a worldwide movement to work less and earn more? Author Tim Ferriss was rebuffed 26 times before he found a publisher willing to take him on.
- Stephen King's first novel, *Carrie*, was turned down 30 times. King was so frustrated he chucked his manuscript into the trash. His wife fished it out and encouraged him to submit it just one more time.
- JK Rowling suffered countless rejections before scoring a hit with the *Harry Potter* series. She's now one of the richest people in Britain.

I think rejection is extra hard on writers because writing is so personal that it feels like we're being rejected as human beings when someone doesn't like our work. But take heart that the rich and famous have been where you are right now, fielding no-thank-yous left and right, and the reason they succeeded is they realized rejection is not personal—it's a business decision made by another person on completely subjective grounds. And then, they kept trying.

In the D-I-A Plan Worksheet for this Desire, you'll have a chance to brainstorm on what type of writing you want to try, and where and when you'll make it a reality. Want to go pro? You'll find more details on how to turn your passion into a side business in Desire #9, *Start a Side Hustle.*

Desire #8: *Become Well-Read*

Being well-read means different things to different people, but the general definition is "knowledgeable and informed as a result of extensive reading." Knowledgeable and informed? Sign me up! This D-I-A Desire is about hitting the books—and newspapers, and magazines—and improving your life in the process.

Why this Desire?

Ah, reading! It's amazing how much good can come out of what looks to your cat like you sitting and staring intently at an inanimate object for no reason. The benefits of reading include:

Helping you destress. When you lose yourself in an amazing story, your problems seem to fall into oblivion. Sounds perfect for someone blasting toward a D-I-A life!

Giving you a new perspective. Reading a novel by Indonesia's number one author, browsing the editorials in your local paper, or delving into a magazine from a part of the newsstand you never bothered perusing before offers you a glimpse of how the other 7.3 billion people on this planet think.

Keeping your brain healthy. This article title on the ABC News website says it all: "Reading, Chess May Help Fight Alzheimer's." Reading also improves your short-term memory and boosts your focus and concentration.

Teaching you cool stuff. Whether you want to know more about investing or feudal Japan, you can learn about it by reading.

Keeping you current. Newspapers (online or print), news curators (like TheSkimm.com), and books that tackle current events keep you abreast of what's going on in our world.

Giving you something to talk about. If you're a voracious reader, you'll always have an icebreaker, and never be standing alone at a cocktail party with a sweating glass in a sweating hand, afraid to approach people because you don't know what to say.

Making you nicer. Research from the *Journal of Personality and Individual Differences* shows that reading fiction increases your empathy and prosocial behavior, which is all that nice stuff like sharing, helping, volunteering, and donating.

Plays well with your other D-I-A Desires. *Do More Stuff with the People You Love*: Read *Harry Potter* to your kids. *Volunteer*: See the point just above this one. *Write*: More reading leads to better writing. *Gain Mad Skills*: When you're learning a new skill, reading is a good complement to practicing. *Grow Your Spiritual Practice*: Religious texts, spiritual books, self-help books…need I say more?

No matter what kind of reading you do, you'll learn and grow at a crazy-fast pace if you do a lot of it. Already a voracious reader? Try switching up your genre or topic of choice.

The value match:

If your top value is:	Here's how you can make a match.
Influence	The more you know, the better position you're in to become an influencer—a person with so much knowledge on a topic that others seek her out, or that she affects others' decisions.
Happiness	As mentioned above, reading can make you calmer, healthier, and nicer—all prerequisites to happiness.
Challenge	Choose challenging reading topics, or read a genre that's unfamiliar to you; for example, if you normally read science fiction, try narrative nonfiction. If your nightstand is stacked with the latest bestsellers, dive into some classics.
Poise	Being well-read boosts your confidence, which is a key ingredient in poise.

What do you mean by *Become Well-Read*?

Above I mentioned that *well-read* is defined as "knowledgeable and informed as a result of extensive reading." But knowledgeable and informed about what, exactly? That's up to you. I read a lot of military sci-fi, so does a familiarity with military sci-fi authors and a knowledge of what FTL stands for count? If you read all the classics required in high schools today, would that qualify? How about if you read *The Economist* or *The New Yorker* every week?

You're a smart woman, so I'll leave that decision up to you. I think you'll agree that reading manga or gossip rags six hours per day does not make a person well-read in the conventional sense, but as always, your D-I-A Plan is your own!

Stuck? Here are some suggested Goals:

Level 1: Read five classic novels you should have read in high school but didn't.

Level 2: Choose a broad topic, from current events to pop science to religion, and devote a month to reading books and magazines about it.

Level 3: Organize a book club based around books you've always wanted to read.

How do I make it happen?

This is a fun one because *well-read* has such a broad definition—but at the same time, this broadness can cause you to freeze in place in the middle of Barnes & Noble, not knowing whether to head for the New Fiction tables or the Art, Architecture, and Photography section. Here are some ways to figure it all out:

Look for lists. Overwhelmed by the enormous variety of the written word? Seek out lists other readers have helpfully compiled for you, like "20 Classic And Important Books That Will Make You Feel Well-Read, Even If They're The Only Ones You Read" on *Bustle* magazine's website. Other options include the *New York Times* bestseller list, Amazon.com's top selling categories, and lists compiled by indie bookstores.

Pinpoint your weakness. Where do you feel you've missed the boat, reading-wise? For example, I've got many of the classics of

Russian literature under my belt, but have slacked on non-Russian classics, and have always been under-informed in terms of the news. *The Complete Works of Jane Austen*, and *The Bronte Sisters—The Complete Novels* (each just a couple bucks on Kindle!), and a subscription to *The Economist* and TheSkimm.com have helped remedy that.

Stretch yourself. Don't think you have to spend all your time poring over Shakespeare to be well-read. Mysteries, thrillers, and graphic novels; poetry, religious texts, and literary journals; history, politics, and news; magazines, newspapers, and e-books—it's all fair game!

Pick your favorite. You can be well-read in a broad sense, or well-read on a certain topic. If you want to read every book, article, and blog post written about the Revolutionary War, then go for it!

Read on the cheap. If you're reading a lot, books can get pretty pricy. A new hardcover can set you back 30 bucks, and e-books from traditional publishers run as high as 14 dollars and up! Don't forget we have that lovely institution called a library; book swaps and second-hand book stores abound; thrift shops often carry books; Kindle has a lending library; indie authors often offer their books for free or for 99 cents on Amazon to get their names out there; and many communities hold giant book sales. At the annual book sale near us, on the last day you can fill an entire bag with books for five dollars.

Carry a book. Always have a book on you, whether it's a print copy, on an e-reader, or on your phone, so you can read while standing in line, cooling your heels in a waiting room, and so on.

Be random. Why not just wander around the bookstore, an online bookseller, or the local magazine stand, pick up whatever looks interesting to you, and read it? If the tips above help you, great…but you don't need to stick to a list, a theme, or anything else in order to be well-read. Let your gut guide you, and you'll become well-read in ways you'd never considered before.

Your D-I-A Plan Worksheet for this Desire will give you a chance to think about what you'd love to read more of, and how to work more reading into your schedule.

Desire #9: *Start a Side Hustle*

Whether you have a day job that doesn't rock your world, or don't work outside the home at all, here's your chance to build a business to earn extra cash doing what you love. And even if you enjoy your day job, or already own a business doing what you're most passionate about, this is an opportunity to stretch yourself and try something new.

Why this Desire?

As part of your D-I-A life, I want you to do what you love, get your brilliance out there into the world to help other people, create value, and reap the returns from that value. A side business helps you pad your bank account, giving you a sense of self-reliance and the spare cash to go after the rest of your D-I-A Desires. And finally, this is something many of the women I talked to wished they were doing!

The value match:

If your top value is:	Here's how you can make a match.
Achievement	Starting a side business is all about achievement! Do a great job and you'll achieve raving fans, money, new opportunities, awards, and more.
Security	Despite the cries from your Aunt Martha that you must have a full-time job for security, you're actually a lot more secure having a side gig or even a full-time freelance business. Your day job employer can turn off 100% of your income without warning, but as a business owner you typically have multiple clients. So even if you lose one you still have others, and you can always find more.

Trustworthiness	Business owners run into a lot of ethical gray areas. A customer accidentally overpaid you. The portrait you painted is not up to your usual standards, but you're tired, and the client will never know the difference. The IRS will never know about your house-cleaning gig because you're paid under the table. A side business is a chance to put your trustworthiness to the test, and to show the world you're a stand-up kind of woman.
Fame	Want to be loved and adored by the masses? Be amazing at any business you start, and it can happen. Your catering business, modeling gig, graphic design service, or dance classes could turn into superstardom if you're so good that a magazine editor or TV producer seeks you out.

What do you mean by *Start a Side Hustle*?

Your side hustle could actually be a side business, meaning something you do part-time to bring in spare cash, or it could be a business you hope to turn into a full-time gig so you can quit your job. I'm not picky.

As for what kind of side business to launch, the options are limitless. For example, depending on your skills, your interests, the laws in your area, and your ability to learn a new trade, you could:

- Sell your crafts on Etsy.
- Become a freelance writer.
- Pet sit or walk dogs.
- Become a personal trainer.
- Buy and resell products on eBay.
- Bake and decorate cakes, cookies, or cupcakes.
- Clean houses or business offices.
- Do home repairs.
- Garden.

- Offer proofreading or editing services.
- Tutor.
- Become a virtual assistant.
- Start blogging, then sell ads on your site or affiliate-sell products to your readers.
- Give music lessons.
- Do graphic design.
- Become an interior decorator.
- Do web design.
- Take photos.
- Become a social media manager.
- Rent out an extra room in your house on Airbnb.
- Do bookkeeping or accounting.
- Start a home inspection service.
- Teach online classes.
- Tailor and/or alter clothes.
- Model.
- Become a personal chef.
- Give walking tours of your city.
- Paint portraits of people or pets.
- DJ at parties.
- Become an event or wedding planner.
- Do stand-up comedy.
- Run errands.
- Translate.
- House sit.
- Become a personal shopper.
- Build apps.
- Become a clown or magician for kids' birthday parties.
- Write resumes and cover letters.
- Become a business or life coach.

I need to stop here because I could list opportunities all day. If you can do something not everyone can do, someone out there will be willing to pay you to do it for them.

Stuck? Here are some suggested Goals:

Level 1: Create a product or service to sell to your friends via word of mouth, Facebook, and flyers.

Level 2: Sell items you create, from crafts to cookies, in local shops, or sell your services locally with print or online classified ads, flyers, door-to-door sales, and so on.

Level 3: Start a full-fledged side business with a company name, website and all the trappings.

How do I make it happen?

Starting a side business is *easy,* but not *simple.* In its purest essence, you tell someone, "I'll do X for $Y," and then they say yes, and then you do it. And you can certainly do that, and then learn along the way! That's how I started a freelance translation business back before the internet was a thing, and was eventually offered a full-time translation job for an amount of money that, at the time, made my eyes bug out. But if you want to go about your D-I-A Goal in a more measured way, and learn the ins and outs of running a successful side hustle, here's how to start:

Look inside. What special skill or passion do you have that you wish you could share with the world? Look into your education, training, hobbies, and job experiences. You may be surprised at the skills you have that you never gave a second thought to. For example, maybe you worked in retail as a teen and were pretty darned good at it, or you're so funny you could make people pee their pants laughing at a funeral, or you really enjoyed the business class you took in college even though your major was in English literature, or you were brought up in a bilingual home. Match up your newly-discovered skills or interests with one of the opportunities you read about in the many lists online, and *voila*! Side gig!

Read lists. Not sure what kind of side business you want to start? Google *side business ideas,* and you'll be inundated with list after list of potential opportunities.

Spread the word. As long as you're not afraid your employer will find out about your side hustle and hand you a pink slip, let everyone know you're now doing X: Taking family photos, blogging, selling cupcakes, creating book trailers, whatever. This is one time where Facebook can actually be helpful: You may be able to build a decent customer base among your friends and family, and if you're ready for more, they can spread the word and introduce you to other potential customers.

Don't get arrested. Check the laws and regulations in your area and your industry. Depending on your side business and where you live, you may need to apply for a business license, earn a certification, and so on.

Get expert advice. You may be an amazing painter or gifted life coach, but most self-employed people fall down when it comes to the actual *business* side of things. Determining who your market is, marketing, advertising, offering stellar customer service, negotiating, networking, and figuring out finances, certifications, and taxes are critical activities for a business owner. Try joining your local Chamber of Commerce, asking an entrepreneur friend for advice, attending local meetings for small business owners, or hiring a business coach, so you can blast through the learning curve and start raking it in.

Act first, plan later. A common issue I see with the writers I coach is that they won't start marketing their services until they have the perfect website. And now they finally have a website, but realize they need to brush up on their punctuation skills. And now they've done *that*, but need to learn the art of the pitch. The need for more skills, equipment, learning…it never ends because obsessing over these needs keeps you from actually getting off your butt, starting your business, and possibly making a fool of yourself. My advice is to start marketing your business even before you're ready. When you land your first sale, then you can scramble to make it work. "Oh, jeez, now I have to figure out how to write this case study/make these 100 cupcakes/plan this event I just sold to a client!"

Develop a thick skin. What if you start a side business and fail? Welcome to the world of just about every business owner on the planet. Don't consider failure *failure*—consider it information gathering. Congratulations! You discovered something that won't work, so now you can try something else that might. Case in point: As a freelance writer, I've been rejected well over 500 times in my career, and yet here I am, still standing.

In the D-I-A Worksheet for this Desire, you'll have plenty of space to figure out what you want to do, how you want to do it, how to make the time, and how to make it happen.

Desire #10: *Gain Mad Skills*

Deep within your soul, there's probably something you wish you knew how to do, but you always had some excuse for not learning how to do it—whether it's mastering a party trick to impress your friends, learning to speed read or touch type, becoming a wine expert, picking up a foreign language, or learning to knit. Here's where you'll finally bust the excuses and make your hidden dream a reality!

Why this Desire?

Doing it all is about doing, seeing, experiencing, and creating everything you desire. Learning a new skill will boost your confidence, increase your self-reliance, and let you master something you can show to the world and say, "I did this."

This Desire also helps with many other D-I-A Desires. *Travel*: Learn the language of the country you're traveling to. *Start a Side Hustle*: Learn to DJ so you can start a business mixing and scratching at parties and clubs. *Entertain*: Learn how to pair the perfect wines with your meals. Finally, in talking with women about their D-I-A Desires, learning a new skill is one that came up over and over again.

The value match:

If your top value is:	Here's how you can make a match.
Love	Develop a skill that will help you show others some love: Learn to knit so you can create cozy socks for your friends. Pick up flower arranging so you can give people homemade bouquets just because. Take a class in loving-kindness meditation.

Recognition	Get good at a skill, and you're sure to be recognized for it!
Passion	Pick a skill that will enhance your ability to do something you're passionate about. Movie buff? Learn how to create your own films. Animal lover? Take a class in dog grooming. Health nut? Learn how to make your own fermented foods.
Citizenship	What skills would help you win the good citizenship award? Could you learn to bake so you can bring goodies to the veteran's hospital? Could learn to sing so you can croon away at the senior center?

What do you mean by *Gain Mad Skills*?

I mean something you've always wanted to know how to do, a skill that would enhance your life or career, or a skill that will make you, and possibly other people, feel great. Here's just a tiny sampling of the skills you can learn:

- A musical instrument.
- A foreign language: Dutch, Japanese, Bosnian, Urdu...whatever!
- Knitting.
- Party tricks.
- Card tricks.
- Juggling.
- Video editing.
- Chinese brush painting.
- Hop-hop dancing.
- Yoga.
- Sewing.
- Magic.
- Singing.
- Writing.

- French cooking.
- Bird watching.
- Meditation.
- Kite flying.
- In-line skating.
- Coding.
- Speed reading.
- Podcasting.
- Public speaking.
- Personal finances.
- Shorthand. (Yes, people still use this!)
- Photography.

This list could fill a whole book. Possible skills you can learn range from the purely mental to the mostly physical, and they can be career-related, hobby-related, or just-because-I-feel-like-it. They can help or entertain others, or be something you do only for yourself. And your learning process could involve taking a class, pursuing a certificate, going to college for a degree, or just reading books on a topic you're curious about.

However, be sure you choose a quantifiable Goal, meaning you know when you're done developing the skill. There's always more to learn—even professionals keep training and learning—so knowing your end point is crucial. For example, if your Goal is to learn yoga, maybe you know you're done with this Goal when you've moved up to advanced level classes, or are able to flawlessly perform five difficult yoga poses.

Stuck? Here are some suggested Goals:

Level 1: Learn to knit and knit a scarf in one month.

Level 2: Learn a foreign language and have a ten-minute conversation with a native speaker of that language.

Level 3: Learn to play an instrument or sing, and hold an informal performance for your family and friends.

How do I make it happen?

Time to put on your thinking cap—or if you were in Japan, you would tie a *hachimaki* around your head, signaling that you're about to focus your butt off on choosing and building a new skill. Here's how:

Read up. If you want to learn something, chances are there's a book, e-book, blog, or magazine devoted to teaching you how. Buy a bunch, read, try out the tips.

Watch YouTube. YouTube is bursting with videos that can teach you anything from coding, to how to apply makeup for the camera, to how to fix a balky washing machine. Don't think these videos are lame replacements for "real" learning. The winner of the first season of *Project Runway Junior* was a 14-year-old girl whose designs could make you cry with happiness, and she learned to sew by watching YouTube tutorials.

Take a class. Many colleges and community centers offer adult education classes that are held in the evenings, on topics ranging from acting to nutrition to bridge. Prices are typically fairly low, and some classes are free!

Want to take a class without leaving your home? Try taking an inexpensive course through a site like Udemy.com or MasterClass.com. At MasterClass, you learn from luminaries in their fields for just $90: Tennis from Serena Williams, writing from James Patterson, photography from Annie Leibovitz, and so on. Coursera.com offers courses in everything from grammar and punctuation to machine learning from universities like Stanford, Princeton, and Johns Hopkins, at prices ranging from $30 to $120. Finally, many universities offer free podcasts of their courses.

Looking to learn a more hands-on skill? Craftsy.com and Creativebug.com offer hundreds of free and cheap classes and tutorials, from knitting, weaving, and crocheting to woodworking, gardening, and drawing.

Use an app. Seek out apps that will let you learn a new skill wherever you are and whenever you have the time. For example, my husband used the free app Duolingo to pick up German, and the Star Chart app for Android ($2.99) helps you learn astronomy: Just point your device at the sky and the app will tell you exactly what you're looking at.

Get schooled. If the skill you want to pick up is more complicated than what you can learn by reading a book or taking a single class, or you want to go deeper into the subject or even turn it into a new career, consider earning a college degree, attending a trade school, or earning a certificate. Plumbing, acupuncture, physical therapy, coaching, and interior design are just a few skills that you could go to school for. Luckily for us, many certificate programs take place online and via phone these days, and some universities offer online degrees as well—though you need to make sure the university is reputable and accredited.

Ask a friend. Know someone who knows what you want to know? Ask them to teach it to you. For example, several years ago, a friend-of-a-friend taught me how to knit. You may have buddies who can help you learn to play the drums, line dance, bake—you'll be surprised at how talented your friends are!

Okay, you're all fired up to stuff that beautiful brain full of new knowledge. Head on over to the *Gain Mad Skills* D-I-A Worksheet to work out the details.

Desire #11: *Grow Your Spiritual Practice*

Want to feel awesome? (Is anyone out there actually saying no? I didn't think so.) Starting or growing a spiritual practice can help an awful lot with that. Don't worry—you don't need to buy prayer beads, chant a mantra, or do anything that feels awkward to you. Read on for details and options.

Why this Desire?

A spiritual practice is one more activity that can count toward doing it all, but at the same time, it assists in your D-I-A practice by keeping you healthy, balanced, and whole. A spiritual practice:

Lifts your mood. A regular practice of meditation, prayer, yoga, or whatever spiritual activities you choose, helps you experience more joy and happiness, and keeps negative events from impacting you as much as they normally would.

Helps you solve problems. When you present your mind with a problem, and then go into your spiritual practice—whatever that is to you—often you'll come out of it with a new perception or a new awareness of how to deal with the issue. And even if you don't, you're likely to feel less stressed and upset by the problem.

Keeps you healthy. According to research by the University of Minnesota, "People who practice a religion or faith tradition are less likely to smoke or drink, commit a crime, or become involved in violent activity, and they are more likely to engage in preventative habits like wearing seatbelts and taking vitamins."

Helps you live longer. People with a higher spirituality and religiosity value have an 18% reduction in mortality, which is about the same reduction experienced by people who eat more fruits and veggies.

Complements your other D-I-A Desires. Regular volunteering can count as a spiritual practice, depending on how you approach it. Holding a meditation or prayer group in your home counts as entertaining. Your D-I-A Desire *Travel* may have a spiritual bent as well; for example, when we visited Japan, our son spent a meditative hour in a temple copying a Buddhist text with a brush and ink.

And of course, in talking with women about their D-I-A Desires, many expressed a wish to grow in a spiritual way, which is why it's included here.

Not a newbie? If you already have a spiritual practice, this is a chance to explore different ones or expand the one you already have.

The value match:

If your top value is:	Here's how you can make a match.
Acceptance	A spiritual practice is all about acceptance. Accepting others as they are, accepting a greater power into your life, accepting yourself as you are, accepting the present moment.
Commitment	That's easy: Commit to a regular spiritual practice!

Frugality	A regular habit of meditation, praying, journaling, or any other spiritual practice can help you become less attached to material objects like the cars, jewelry, and designer handbags we all want so badly, but that cost lots of money.
Intimacy	A spiritual practice can improve your relationships. You become more tolerant of other people's quirks, lose your hair-trigger temper, and become more loving.

What do you mean by *Grow Your Spiritual Practice*?

I'm not even going to get into the mess of attempting to explain the difference between spirituality and religion. But I will tell you that spirituality is simply *the quality of being spiritual*, whatever that means to you. Anything that makes you feel in touch with yourself, the universe, or your higher power of choice is fair game. Any of these activities below, and many more, can qualify:

- Prayer.
- Sitting in nature.
- Reading spiritual books or religious texts.
- Meditation.
- Attending gatherings of like-minded practitioners, whether it's a prayer group or a meditation group.
- Activities like yoga, tai chi, and mindful walking.
- Attending a place of worship.
- Visualization.
- Journaling.
- Anything that gets you in the zone, from running to baking.

You can probably think of many activities I haven't included on this list.

Stuck? Here are some suggested Goals:

Level 1: Read four religious or spiritual texts in one month.
Level 2: Test drive a religious or spiritual group for one month, such as a prayer group, a meditation group, or a place of worship.
Level 3: Commit to a regular, ongoing spiritual practice; for example, join a church, sign up for yoga teacher training, or set aside 30 minutes every day to meditate.

How do I make it happen?

There are no rules, thank goodness, so no one will be standing over you barking, "Pray!" or "Downward dog, *now*!" That said, starting and developing a spiritual practice can be overwhelming because there are so many options. Here are some ideas for easing into the best practice for you.

Experiment. If you're not sure where to start, experiment until you find a practice that speaks to you. Look online for different Meetup groups, classes, ceremonies, places of worship, and so on. Read books on different spiritual practices, and texts from different religions, and see if one strikes you as just right.

Talk to your friends. Ask your friends if they have a spiritual practice and if so, what it involves. If something they do resonates with you, ask if you can join them. For example, a friend of mine recently invited me to attend her non-denominational prayer group. Another friend was invited by a Jewish buddy to attend a service at her synagogue... atheists welcome!

Start small. You don't need to start chanting on a meditation cushion an hour a day or racing through religious texts by the dozen. Why not start with doing five minutes of meditation, or reciting a short prayer, or writing one page in your journal daily?

Get what you need. Decide what tools you want to start your spiritual practice, and then gather them up. Examples include a meditation cushion, incense, a yoga mat, walking shoes, soothing music and earphones, religious or spiritual books, and a beautiful journal and pen. Of course, you don't necessarily need *anything*. Visiting a place of worship, meditating, walking, yoga, and sitting in nature can all be done for free, with no special tools at all.

Make it a habit. Whatever you choose to do, make it a part of your regular schedule: Daily meditation, church on Sunday, a weekly prayer group, or a morning nature hike, for example.

Listen to yourself. Your body, mind, and spirit know what you need, if you'll only listen. Maybe one day you get the sense you don't need your regular journaling time, but you do need a mindful walk. Go with it...there is no wrong here!

Go bigger. If you already have a regular spiritual practice, this Desire is your chance to kick it up a notch. Can you try something new, or do more of what you're already practicing?

Check out the D-I-A Worksheet for this Desire for a chance to explore what a spiritual practice means to you, and figure out a practice and a schedule that will make you feel your awesomest.

Desire #12: *Do More Stuff with the People You Love*

I saved the most important D-I-A Desire for last. As you'll learn below, this is the one that can impact your life, and the lives of those around you, the most.

Why this Desire?

I'd say this is the number one thing anyone can do to make their lives happier, brighter, and more joyful, and to create these same feelings in their loved ones.

At the end of their lives, people's top regrets tend to center around relationships, how they treated others, and how much or how little they did with their friends and family. For example, *Forbes* ran an article called "The 25 Biggest Regrets in Life—What's Yours?" Here are six of those 25 top regrets:

- Working too much at the expense of family and friendships.
- Not going on trips with family and friends.
- Letting their marriage break down.
- Not teaching their kids to do more.
- Not spending enough time with their kids.
- Not visiting a dying friend before they passed away.

Lifehack, similarly, ran a piece on the "Top 7 Regrets of People Who Are Dying." Two of them are:

- "I wish I had touched more lives and inspired more people."
- "I wish I had been a better partner or parent."

Finally, this D-I-A Desire fits in perfectly with many of the others—you can travel, compete in an athletic event, volunteer, be spiritual, start a side business, or even write along with your friends and family. My husband and I have been freelance writing together for the last 20 years!

So…that's why this Desire.

The value match:

If your top value is:	**Here's how you can make a match.**
Bravery	Reworking your priorities and your life to spend more time with the people you love is brave in a world where so many people find it easier and safer to work and attend school in separate places, and then zone out on individual pursuits in the evening.
Outrageousness	Do something silly with your loved ones! For my 47th birthday, I invited all my friends to go see *Zoolander 2* at a recline-and-dine theater, and then we all gathered at my house for cake.
Abundance	Doing more stuff with the people you love leads to an abundance of fun, an abundance of love, and an abundance of memories.
Learning	You wouldn't believe what you can learn from being with and listening to your friends and family, from new facts to new skills to new mindsets.

What do you mean by *Do More Stuff with the People You Love?*

I mean, do more stuff with more people! I don't care what it is, or who you do it with. You can start with the three Levels of Goals listed below, but hopefully the previous 11 D-I-A Desires have given you some experiences and ideas for what you'd love to share with others. Here are just a few examples:

- Take your kids to an art museum, and bring crayons and sketchbooks so they can draw what they see.
- Invite a friend to join you at a function at your church.
- Volunteer for Meals on Wheels with your partner.
- Host a giant family reunion for all those cousins, aunts, and uncles you haven't seen in years.
- Invite a family of refugees over for Thanksgiving dinner with your own family.
- Visit out-of-state friends you haven't seen in forever, or invite them to come visit you.
- Take your family to the movies, the zoo, the library, the state capitol, the park, or the café.
- Homeschool your kids.
- Go on regular date nights with your partner.
- Pop some corn and watch a movie at home with your family or friends.
- Ask your parents and in-laws over for Sunday brunch.
- Take classes at a clown college with your best friend.
- Take an ailing, down-in-the-dumps friend to a comedy show.
- Schedule a girls' nights out.
- Gather a team of friends and family to run a 5k, and dress in a theme.
- Yank your kids out of school for a year and travel the country in an RV.

Hopefully that will get the wheels turning in your head. There are so many options for doing more stuff with the ones you love, it could fill a book. Or three.

Stuck? Here are some suggested Goals:

Level 1: Schedule four fun outings with at least one loved one in one month. Get creative!

Level 2: Organize a regular weekly date night, girls' night out, game group, or other gathering.

Level 3: Host a reunion of far-flung family or friends that includes projects, games, and events you can do as a group.

How do I make it happen?

First, don't over-think it! This one is all about having fun, sharing great experiences, and creating memories, so if you turn it into some big, scary goal, that defeats the purpose. But if you're not quite sure where to begin, here are some strategies to try:

Know your peeps. Figure out who you want to be with most, and who you wish you were spending more time with. *Do not* add people to your list if you aren't that into them out of a feeling of guilt. So who makes *your* list? Your best friend from college? Your partner? Kids? Far-flung relatives? Parents? Local buddies?

Ask your peeps. If you're stumped as to what to do with all these people, here's a novel idea: Ask them. Text your best friend and tell her you'd like to see her more, and what would she enjoy doing most? Hold a family meeting and let everyone contribute ideas for what they'd love to do more of.

Get creative. While those date nights, movie nights at home, and coffees with friends are all perfect ways to do more with the people you love, the activities and events that will create the most and best memories are those that are outside your normal routine—the trapeze lessons, volunteer missions, trips, arcade game tournaments, and so on.

Schedule your fun. Don't wait for time to miraculously open up in your schedule to squeeze this D-I-A Desire into. Instead, *make* the time to do things with your loved ones, and stick this time into your calendar, otherwise it will never happen. A Taiwanese study in the *Journal of Happiness Studies* found a positive relationship between free time management and quality of life. Sounds good to me!

This is it—the end of your D-I-A Plan—and this Goal is the biggest, baddest, hardest-yet-easiest, most important one. On the D-I-A Worksheet for this Desire, you can write out your plans for doing things you love with people you love. Have fun!

Chapter 34

What's Next?

If you're reading this chapter, you should be done with your D-I-A Plan. And you're probably wondering what happens once you make it through all that learning, doing, experiencing, creating, seeing, and accomplishing.

You're probably also feeling exhausted, worn out, brain dead—and yet excited to do even more. Stretching yourself and taking on new adventures becomes addictive…in a *good* way.

Now's the time to go to the Recap Worksheet included in the bonus downloads and free-write about the experience using the prompts there. You'll be able to figure out what you learned from your experience, what you enjoyed, what you hated, what you want to do more of, and what totally new adventures you want to add to your life.

Then, create a new Plan and start afresh! If you enjoyed your D-I-A experience, you can keep it up forever.

Chapter 35

OMG!

OMG! You're now a woman who does it all. You look great and live in a home you love; savor closer connections and fun memories with your friends and family; know yourself better through your writing and spiritual practice; boast mad skills and extensive knowledge; and have earned your *Kick-Ass Woman* badge by running a business and giving your all in an athletic event.

I'm proud to know you, and you should be proud of yourself, too.

Onward!

Acknowledgements

I'd like to thank the many people who made this book possible and helped me make it as good as I possibly could. Let's start with Diana Burrell, my business partner in *Renegade Writer Press* who helped me shape the book and the Plan, offered encouragement, and was not afraid to give me the real deal on what worked and what didn't work.

This book wouldn't be nearly as good without my wonderful Beta Readers. A big thanks to Barb Morris, Beth Terrell, Candace Larry, Elisabeth Rossman, Emma Murphy-Smith, Farrah Blakely, H. Josée Allard, Jennifer Lawler, Kurt Buss, Liane Bonin, Linda Elmer, Lynn Jarrett, Mary Ann Bella, Melanie Nicsinger, Milena Glavonjic, Paula Richey, Rachel Newcomb, Rebecca Esther, Sandy Murphy, Sarah Li Cain, Wendy Strain, and Williesha Morris.

I love all the writers and readers on the *How to Do It All* Facebook Group! They're full of inspiration and ideas. Thank you for being there and contributing.

This book looks so amazingly awesome thanks to proofreader Vince Dickinson, print layout designer Stephanee Killen of Integrative Ink, and cover designer James at GoOnWrite.com.

And of course, thank you to Eric Martin, Traver Martin, Marija Obrenovic, and Janet and Tony Formichelli for bearing with me while I did nothing but work on this book for three months straight, and for your encouragement and help.

Appendix

The Worksheets

You can download a free package of printable Worksheets at:

www.therenegadewriter.com/D-I-AWorksheets

But for those of you who prefer to journal your Plan or make your own Worksheets, this Appendix offers a list of each Worksheet, along with every question or prompt in them.

The Values Checklist

Circle the three values that resonate most with you—the ones that make you feel happy or excited, or even cause you to cry a little with joy. If you have a value that's not included here, just add it into one of the blanks at the end of the list.

After you choose your top three values, head down to the end of the worksheet and brainstorm on what each value means to you.

Abundance
Acceptance
Achievement
Action
Adventure
Art
Authenticity
Authority
Autonomy
Availability
Awareness
Balance
Beauty
Belonging
Boldness
Bravery
Carefulness
Challenge
Charity
Chastity
Citizenship
Clarity
Cleanliness
Comfort
Commitment
Community
Compassion
Competency
Contribution
Creativity
Curiosity
Determination
Fairness
Faith
Fame
Focus
Friendships
Frugality
Fun
Generosity
Gratitude
Growth
Happiness
Heroism
Honesty
Hospitality
Humility
Humor
Impact
Influence
Inner Harmony

Inspiration
Integrity
Intelligence
Intensity
Intimacy
Joy
Justice
Kindness
Knowledge
Leadership
Learning
Liberty
Longevity
Love
Loyalty
Mastery
Maturity
Meaningful Work
Modesty
Moxie
Nature
Nonconformity
Openness
Optimism
Organization
Originality
Outrageousness
Peace
Pleasure
Poise
Popularity
Purity
Reason
Recognition
Relaxation
Religion
Reputation
Respect
Responsibility
Restraint
Rigor
Security
Self-Control
Self-Respect
Sensitivity
Service
Sexiness
Sexuality
Sharing
Simplicity
Sophistication
Spirituality
Stability
Status
Success
Tolerance
Trustworthiness
Wealth
Wisdom

Other value not in the list: ______________
Other value not in the list: ______________
Other value not in the list: ______________

What do my values mean to me?

Value: ___________
What it means to me:

Value: ___________
What it means to me:

Value: ___________
What it means to me:

Tolerations List

Here's where you can list all the little things that are bugging you and getting in the way of your D-I-A Desires. Try to reach 100—it's not as hard as you'd think. I've provided categories to make the brainstorming process easier for you. Add more tolerations as they come up, and cross off ones you've taken care of.

My tolerations are:

Health tolerations:
Home tolerations:
Career tolerations:
Equipment and appliance tolerations:
Environment tolerations:
Time tolerations:
Relationship tolerations:
Finances tolerations:

Killed Tolerations List

Got rid of a toleration? Awesome! Add it here so you can look back on the list occasionally and experience a bump in pride and motivation.

Here are the tolerations I've killed so far. I rock!

To-Don't List

Jot down a list of the obligations and tasks you'll cut out of your life in order to make more time and mental space for your current D-I-A Desire. You can pull from your Tolerations List for this!

Here's what I will no longer be doing as I work on my current D-I-A Desire:

Night-Time Brain Dump List

Each night before bed, list all the problems, issues, and to-dos that are on your mind, so they don't keep you awake all night. In the morning, go through the list with a fresh perspective and take care of, schedule, delete, or delegate the items on it.

What's on my mind tonight:

Rule of Four List

Use this Worksheet whenever you're feeling overwhelmed and want to pare down your to-do list to your top priorities.

Here are the top four things I need to get done today:

1.

2.

3.

4.

Admin Day To-Do List

Use this Worksheet every week to jot down any necessary tasks that aren't in service of your D-I-A Desires, and that you plan to save for your Admin Day.

On my Admin Day, I need to accomplish these tasks:

Did List

Jot down everything you accomplished in the past day—or week, if you don't want to do it daily.

Here are all the tasks, to-dos, and goals I've accomplished. Yay!

Naikan Worksheet

1. *What did I receive from others today?*

2. *What have I given to others today?*

3. *What troubles and difficulties did I cause others today?*

The 12 D-I-A Worksheets and the Blank Desire Worksheet

These Worksheets are all the same, except that you'll write the name of the current Desire on the top of your sheet. As a reminder, the 12 Desires are:

1. Love Your Looks
2. Travel
3. Create an Amazing Home
4. Cross a Finish Line
5. Entertain
6. Volunteer
7. Write
8. Become Well-Read
9. Start a Side Hustle
10. Gain Mad Skills
11. Grow your Spiritual Practice
12. Do More Stuff with the People You Love

If you want to replace a D-I-A Desire with one of your own, use this Worksheet and write in the name of whatever Desire you choose.

What does this Desire look like to me?

How does this D-I-A Desire fit at least one of the top three personal values I circled on the Values Checklist?

Here's an exercise to help me get unstuck: What if I went after the most outrageous manifestation of this Desire? What would it look like?

Now, what would I do to make these outrageous Goals happen?

How can I apply any of these crazy ideas and tactics to my actual D-I-A Goals?

What if I had to achieve my D-I-A Goals in one month or I would literally die? What would I do to make it happen?

Here's where I'll break it down: What steps do I need to take to get my D-I-A Goal rolling?

Here's exactly where and when I'll take those steps:

Let me schedule these tasks into my calendar right now. ___ *I'm done!*

Let me look into the future and imagine I'm about to do X. If I foresee any obstacles, what can I do right now to make those future obstacles non-issues?

Can I enlist help with my Goal? For example, can I ask a friend or family member, join an online community devoted to this Goal, find a mentor, or hire a pro? Ye______ No______

If so, what kind of help can I enlist?

Brainstorm time! Here's who I'll be asking for help, where to find them, how I'll approach them, and how—if they're hired pros or paid services—I can pay for them.

If someone is watching me on a screen as I work on this D-I-A Goal, how would this person know I'm actually working hard?

How can I automate this D-I-A Goal, or parts the Goal?

If I feel overwhelmed while working on this D-I-A Goal, I'll try these practices to banish the overwhelm and get back to work. (Naikan, meditation, exercise, yoga, a hot bath, etc.)

Here are the top ten tolerations I'll be getting rid of while I work on this D-I-A Goal, and how I'll do it:

1.

2.

3.

4.

5.

6.

7.

8.

9.

10.

Further thoughts/inspirations/brainstorms:

The Missing Desire Worksheet

If you've determined that you dislike one of the D-I-A Desires, but aren't sure what Desire to replace it with, use this Worksheet to brainstorm one.

What's missing in my life?

What activities and experiences make me feel confident, assured, and joyful?

What would I do if I won the Powerball lottery?

What would I do if no one was judging me?

What do I wish I were doing that I'm not?

If I were on my deathbed, looking back on my life, what would I regret not *doing?*

What am I doing now that I wish I were doing more of?

What do I wish I could create?

*My new Desire:*__________________________

The Recap Worksheet

Save this for after you complete the D-I-A Plan! Use this Worksheet to free-write about your D-I-A experience and figure out where you want to go from here.

Here are the Desires I've completed:

I loved working on these Desires:

I disliked working on these Desires:

These Desires made me feel just meh*:*

This was the number one best Desire, that had the most lasting positive results in my life:

Here's how my life has changed since starting the D-I-A Plan, for better and for worse:

My D-I-A Plan affected my relationships in this way:

My D-I-A Plan affected my health in this way:

My D-I-A Plan affected my mood in this way:

My D-I-A Plan affected my career in this way:

My biggest wins during this experience were:

My biggest excuses when going for my D-I-A Desires were:

I wish I had done this differently:

If I were to do it all over again choosing 12 completely new Desires or Goals, they would be:

1.

2.

3.

4.

5.

6.

7.

8.

9.

10.

11.

12.

I want to keep Doing It All: Yes______ No_______

What's the next step for me?

About the Author

Linda Formichelli is a freelance writer living in the Raleigh area with her writer husband, ballet-dancing son, three rescue cats, and frequently an exchange student as well. She's written for over 150 magazines, from *Pizza Today* to *Woman's Day*; authored and co-authored over a dozen books, including *The Renegade Writer* and *Becoming a Personal Trainer for Dummies* (which she always thought made it sound like the reader was training dummies); and guest posted at top blogs like *Copyblogger*, *Tiny Buddha*, and *Write to Done*.

Linda is also the co-founder of *Renegade Writer Press*, which publishes books for writers and other smart people.

More from Renegade Writer Press

Like what you read here? Then you'll love our other books, including:

Commit: How to Blast Through Problems & Reach Your Goals Through Massive Action

The Renegade Writer: A Totally Unconventional Guide to Freelance Writing Success

Write Your Way Out of the Rat Race...And Step Into a Career You Love

You can find all these books and more at www.therenegadewriter.com. Come on over!

54726956R00134

Made in the USA
Lexington, KY
26 August 2016